Provençal Series

General Editor, Peter Whigham

THE MUSIC OF THE TROUBADOURS

Provençal Series

amo ut intellegam

Volume 1

THE MUSIC OF THE TROUBADOURS

edited by Peter Whigham

I: THE MUSIC OF THE TROUBADOURS

II: NEUF CHANSONS DE TROUBADOURS

III: GUILHEM IX—TEXTS AND TRANSLATION

Ross-Erikson

Santa Barbara

ISBN 0–915520–13–3

The Music of the Troubadours.

   (Provençal series ; v. 1)
   Bibliography: p. 193.
   Includes index.
   1. Troubadours.   2. Music–History and
criticism–Medieval, 400–1500.   3. Songs,
Provençal–History and criticism.   4. Songs,
Provençal.   5. Provençal poetry. I. Whigham,
Peter. II. Guillaume IX, Duke of Aquitaine,
1071–1127. Les chansons. English & Provençal.
III. Series.
ML182.M95   784'.3'09449   79–15973

CONTENTS

To
FORD MADOX FORD
&
EZRA POUND
for whom Provence was
one of the sacred places

Lo! Ferlies befalleth where is love-gladness,
'neath moon-sleight in orchard when pierceth love's madness.
Silken the song, spun of air, in the dew,
Tense with the immanent muse,
And coins & castles, heaulmes & politics their song.
Where now are the stones? Where is the bright hair of those women?
Gone, all, the long-gone dead among.

from Homage to Ezra Pound,

P.W.

Introduction to the Series

The Music of the Troubadours is the first volume of Ross-Erikson's *Provençal Series* and sets the pattern to be followed by subsequent volumes. Each volume will contain three parts: a monograph on some background topic, from which the volume will take its title; a selection of poems translated for singing to the original tunes and printed with the music transcribed in modern notation; and a section representing one, or at most two, troubadours, translated *in extenso*, but without the music, either because no music for them exists, or because satisfactory translation for song proved beyond the means of any translator that could be found. There are roughly 250 of the original tunes extant and 2,500 of the poems. The overwhelming emphasis in all literary studies has been precisely that—'literary'. The music has been left to the musicologists. The purpose of the *Provençal Series* is to bring the music and the words—the words translated into English—together again in the context of our modern understanding of twelfth century Provence; and this understanding is not the understanding that prevailed when Dr. Francis Hueffer wrote his book, *The Troubadours* (1878), the first on the subject in either English or American letters.

Although Francis Hueffer was the music critic of the London *Times*, his study is as exclusively literary as any other, but it is still probably the best place for an English-speaking reader to start. Much the same, from a different perspective, could be said of the landmark anthology compiled by Hueffer's brother-in-law,[1] Dante Gabriel Rossetti, called variously, *The Early Italian Poets* and *Dante and his Circle* (1861 & 1874).[2] It traces the effect of Provençal poetry in Dante's Italy and exerted the deepest possible influence on all later English writers in the field, including Pound himself in his earlier phase. Later than these, at the turn of the century, just when Pound was beginning his work, the Rev. H. J. Chaytor produced a number of volumes. They have not, in their given scope, to my knowledge been bettered. Unusually, he touches on the music, and in some detail; he outlines a modest grammar; is good on the genesis of the various forms and their literary significance, and is immensely learned on the way the Provençal model almost at once began to affect the neighbouring parts of Europe.

Pound's contribution in *The Spirit of Romance*, in the numerous poems in *Personae*, the essays in *Make It New*, the *Cavalcanti* volume, and in the key place allotted to 'the matter of Provence' in *The Cantos*, is known literary history. What has remained comparatively unknown has been the contribution he made, in concert with Walter Morse Rummel, in *Neuf Chansons de Troubadours*. 'Without curiosity,' Pound was fond of saying, 'there can be no literature'. It is a sad comment on the lack of curiosity in literary circles that it should have taken upwards of sixty years for any of us to heed Pound's example and follow his pointer.

There were, unfortunately, good reasons for the music being left to the musicologists, and these reasons are outlined in Alejandro Planchart's introduction. Gregorian notation

---

1. Cathy and Lucy Madox Brown, daughters of Ford Madox Brown by different marriages, were the wives, respectively, of Francis Hueffer and William Michael Rossetti.

2. It is worth noting, in passing, that the fine English poet, Sally Purcell, author of a lively book of things Provençal, *vidas*, poems, gossip, has thought it worth her while to prepare a scholarly new edition of the Rossetti volume—without being able to find a publisher for it.

indicated tone but not rhythm. There were no bar lines. Could the musical rhythm of a song be adduced from the prosody of the lyric? Beck, a pioneer in the field, thought it could, and it was on Beck and his whilom partner Aubry, that Pound and Rummel drew. Since then, two men have laboured on transcribing the entire corpus of Troubadour and Trouvère song, Friedrich Gennrich in *Der Musikalische Nachlass der Troubadours* (1958–1965), following Beck's theories, and Hendrik van der Werf in *Trouvères, Melodien*, vol. 1 (1977), radically revising them. Werf's book is the successor to his emminently approachable, though scholarly, *The Chansons of the Troubadours and Trouvères, A Study of the Melodies and their Relation to the Poems* (1972), a volume to be recommended to anyone seriously interested in the subject who may nevertheless feel disinclined to venture into the thornier regions of Mediaeval musicology.

Among general volumes, special mention should be made of three. First, Peter Dronke's *Medieval Latin and the Rise of the European Love-Lyric* (1965), which is particularly interesting on the Provençal love-ethic and its relation to the Christian tradition; second, Robert Briffault's *The Troubadours* (original French edition, 1945), the only non-specialist book to treat in detail the question of Arabic influence, which, it is now clear, was very much greater than our forefathers had contemplated; and third, Ford Madox Ford's *Provence, from Minstrels to the Machine* (1935). Ford was Francis Hueffer's son; his book sums up and puts a period to many of the Victorian and Edwardian attitudes to Provence, at the same time as opening more direct, personal approaches. It was written three years before he died and is in the nature of a testament. Between its two covers he crammed all that he had inherited of Provençal lore from the Hueffer-Rossetti circles of his childhood, and that he had picked up *en route* through his life; for he had lived in Provence, tending, as he put it, his 'parched garden plot', a self-exiled man of letters. The book is an expression of the psychology of a landscape; to tread the roads of Old Provence becomes more than a literary fancy. At the same time as we take possession of the past, *it* is found to be occupying *us*—as in the dialectic of Provençal love. Mistral and his Félibrige, the wild horses of the Camargue, the legend of the Trois Maries, Vogelweide's *Nightingale*, the silent spaces of Mont Ségur, all seem like some kaleidescopic wind machine, whirling in southern sunlight, images of the power of the old Roman province and the forces that continue to pass over it. Ford in his eighty or so titles never wrote better.

Of recent translations, Anthony Bonner's *Songs of the Troubadours* (1972) is remarkable for its extensive notes and commentaries. He also writes of the music, even printing some of the tunes, though untranscribed. Paul Blackburn's long awaited *Proensa* (1978), contains some of the cleanest, most vital renderings in the strictly literary tradition that have yet been done in English. His Marcabru is suitably acerbic. Finally, there is W. D. Snodgrass, who to his great credit has gone whole hog for the music and is doing single-handed (making his own transcriptions as well as translations) what Pound and Rummel did in their *Neuf Chansons*.

For anthologies, Martín de Riquier's *Los Trovadores, Historia, Literaria, y Textos* (1975) stands alone. It runs to three volumes, with a long Introduction, elaborate *apparatus*, and admirable plain prose translations of the *vidas* as well as of the poems. Although no music is printed, mention is made when music exists, and the reader is instructed where to find it and by whom it has been transcribed. The bibliography, a major feat in itself, is recommended to readers of the present series. (The Ross-Erikson bibliographies will be cumulative.)

Mont Ségur, Provençal Series, volume 2, will contain an essay on Mont Ségur, a selection of the lyrics and music of Peire Vidal and Peire Cardenal, and text and translation, with notes, of the extant works of Cercamon and Cabestanh. Volume 3, *Dante's Provence*, will describe the shift the love-ethic underwent from its aristocratic Provençal ambience to that of the bourgeois Tuscan *trecento*; Arnaut Daniel's songs will occupy the second section, and Sordello's poems, the third. Volume 4 will turn to the Arabic component, specifically Ibn Sina's *Treatise on Love*, considered in conjunction with Andreas Capellanus's *De Amore*. Here perhaps we shall find ourselves approaching the heart of the matter: what happens to Arab sufism in a Christian context. The sex instinct, controlled, as Andreas would have it, by intelligence, becomes the path to perfection: woman, not as object of desire, but as instructress of love, mistress for the man of the arts of self-control and the mystic states to be induced thereby, as much a servant of the god of love as, through her, is the man.

Amo ut intellegam, as, pithily, the old Latin tag has it—the epigraph which I have selected for this fresh assault on 'the matter of Provence'. We imitate what we love. And imitation is the first form of learning. But, as Spinoza has observed, 'the love of a thing consists in the understanding of its perfections'. And this also would seem true. So it becomes necessary to amend the tag thus: *Amo ut intellegam, sed intellego ut amem*. I love in order that I may understand, but I understand in order that I may (further) love, the 'understanding' being not intellectual but intuitive, what was then thought of as the way of knowing proper to the Heavenly Hierarchy. The point might escape us today; it would have needed no elaboration in the twelfth century. But it still holds, especially for those of us who, in our thought or work, have the urge to lift the Peire Vidals, Bertran de Borns, Arnaut Daniels out of the dust of their own time and set them four-square, alive and singing in ours. For such as them and for such as us, love is the seed-bed. Were we to find ourselves in our unfallen state, back home in Eden, there would be no need of intellection, 'knowledge *about*': all knowledge would be 'knowledge *of*', direct or angelic knowledge, the knowledge which every artist strives for, the knowledge of the Troubadours. We should see and—*pace*—in their best work, the two fellow-artists to whom this volume is dedicated—we should therefore seem as Angels:

To know by being what one loves.

Peter Whigham
General Editor of *Provençal Series*
Santa Barbara, 1979

THE MUSIC OF THE TROUBADOURS

by

J. B. Beck

Translated from the original French by Timothy Wardell

Introduction by Alejandro Planchart

Foreword by J. B. Beck

Introduction

HE revival of the study of medieval and Renaissance music, which had begun in the last decades of the 19th century as Romanticism's vague nostalgia for a distant past gave way to systematic and scientific study of the bygone cultures, gave rise in the early part of this century to a large number of important studies of the music of the 12th, 13th, and 14th centuries. The most prominent scholars involved in this work were Pierre Aubry and Jean Beck in France, and Friedrich Ludwig, Peter Wagner, and Johannes Wolf in Germany. Their work delved not only into medieval chant and the songs of the troubadours, trouvères, and minnesinger, but also into the many repertories of polyphonic music that grew in the shade of the great cathedrals and monasteries of the central Middle Ages, most notably the extraordinary flowering of music that took place in Paris in the 12th and 13th centuries, and remains, more or less accurately called the School of Notre-Dame.

EAN Beck's *La Musique des Troubadours*, which is being presented here in its first English translation, belongs to that early phase of musical studies. It appeared for the first time in Paris in 1910 as part of the series *Les musiciens célèbres*.[1] At the time of its publication Beck had been involved in a bitter controversy with Pierre Aubry on the matter of who had first formulated what is known as "the modal theory," that is, the view that held that the songs of the troubadours and the trouvères were originally sung not only in fixed meter, but also in one or another of the durational patterns known as "the rhythmic modes," patterns that had risen most clearly in the polyphonic music of the Parisian composers of the late 12th and early 13th centuries.[2] The controversy had unfortunate consequences all around. A jury found in Beck's favor in 1909, but Aubry, disappointed with the decision, pressed on his claims with increased bitterness in a series of writings, and his death in a fencing accident in 1910 has been traditionally connected with the preparations he was making to challenge Beck to a duel. Aubry's death deprived France of one of her most promising young scholars, but it did not stop the controversy, which was further fueled by the claims advanced by Johannes Wolf on behalf of Beck's own teacher at

Strasbourg, Friedrich Ludwig.[3] Beck left France in bitterness in 1911, and his own promising career was severely stifled by the pall of the controversy. With the exception of the facsimile editions of a few trouvère manuscripts, he published little original research for the remainder of his life.[4]

Ironically, the entire controversy centered upon what has turned out to be an unclear honor. Later research and a thorough study of all the troubadour and trouvère manuscripts reveals that the modal theory is based on only a few pieces that appear notated that way in late sources, or on the evidence of the few melodies incorporated into the polyphonic repertory of the 13th century, either as *cantus firmi* or as a quotation in the upper voices of a motet.[5] The impression one gains when examining all of the sources is that indeed, some of the trouvère songs, particularly those of the relatively late trouvères, or those of learned men like Adam de la Halle, who also composed polyphonic works, were occassionally sung and notated in modal rhythm, but that the majority of the trouvère repertory, and all of the troubadour melodies, were set down in a notation that simply conveys no information about the rhythm of the music. Thus the rhythm was probably something that varied from performance to performance, something that contradicts the fixed rhythm assumption that underlies the modal theory.

Nevertheless, it is easy to see why the modal theory, even if now it may be thought of as having been based on a hasty evaluation of the sources, was regarded then as so important, and indeed held to be a significant step in the recovery of this repertory. Musicology was then still a very young science, and though the ground had been broken in the 19th century by a number of important scholars, notably August Wilhelm Ambros (1816–1876) and Charles Edmond Henri de Coussemaker (1805–1876),[6] a truly systematic investigation of the different repertories and their manuscript sources had begun just after the turn of the century, and the main problem facing music historians at the time was the transcription and codification of the vast repertories of medieval and Renaissance music that survived in European libraries.[7] In the field of medieval music it was the polyphonic repertory that loomed the largest and posed the most complex problems, and it was precisely such a repertory that was dominated by the system of modal rhythm, so that in a sense the entire thinking of musical scholars at the time, when it came to matters of 12th or 13th century music, was also dominated by the problems posed by the modal and mensural notations in use during those two centuries. Under such circumstances it is not surprising if Ludwig, Beck, and Aubry would be moving independently towards similar conclusions, so that each would consider himself as the true originator of the modal theory. It is also logical that they could not perceive the theory to be incorrect or at least beset with serious ambiguities, for they were also firmly convinced of the fundamental stylistic unity of all medieval art.

Aubry had begun his studies with monophonic music, both sacred and secular, but by 1906 he had turned his attention to the most important collections of late 13th and early 14th century polyphony, the Montpellier and Bamberg codices, as well as the interpolated copy of *Le Roman de Fauvel*.[8] Ludwig had long been involved in his monumental inventory of the sources of Notre-Dame polyphony and the early motet repertory,[9] and Beck already in his dissertation, *Die Melodien der Troubadours*,[10] had published transcriptions of troubadour and trouvère songs that were essentially in modal rhythm.

The adoption of the rhythmic modes for the transcription of the melodies of the troubadours and the trouvères was based upon an even more fundamental assumption, namely, the idea that the repertories of medieval monophonic song were originally sung in some form of precisely measured rhythm. This assumption was derived from the notation of a few late examples and from the indications found in many manuscripts that a good number of the songs were meant to be danced. Another element that contributed to the acceptance of a definitely measured rhythm for these pieces was the tacit feeling, held by many scholars, that the European traditional music known at the time, mostly French and German folksong, did somehow preserve some of the spirit of the old songs. In any case, the modal theory found a relatively quick and general acceptance, and most transcriptions of this repertory follow it to some extent.

It may be that such an acceptance would have been more cautious if the later studies of European traditional music had been available at the time, but such work as that of Béla Bartók and Zoltán Kodály on eastern European and north African folksong, with its rhythmically free and declamatory styles that Bartók called "parlando rubato," were just being undertaken at the time and were all but unknown to medievalists. In any case, the matter of the rhythm of these songs has been vigorously reopened by Hendrik van der Werf in a series of recent studies.[11] He has emphasized time and again that only a very small number of meolodies were ever set down unequivocally in modal notation, stressing also the relatively late date of these sources, and the enormous variation that the songs show, not only in matters of notation, but also in their melodic shape from one written source to another. This has led him to propose a "declamatory style," for their performance, something akin to the rhythm of a normal recitation of the poetry, but done to the pitches of the melody. Among his most telling arguments against a blanket application of modal rhythm to the entire trouvère repertory are his observations concerning the transmission of the works of Adam de la Halle (fl. 1285), one of the last of the trouvères and a learned musician who also wrote polyphonic *rondeaux* and motets. The main source for Adam's works is Paris, Bibliothèque Nationale, MS. *français* 25,566, which transmits virtually all of his surviving pieces. This manuscript, as well as the other sources, give Adam's polyphonic *rondeaux* and his motets in a notation that clearly indicates the rhythm of the parts, but for the nonophonic songs it uses a notation that simply does not indicate any particular rhythm.

EYOND this, van der Werf has also attempted to show how the writings of Johannes de Grocheo (fl. 1300), the one music theorist who does deal with the music of the trouvères, do not imply, as is often thought, that the music was strictly measured. Indeed, Johannes does speak in this context of a music that was "not precisely measured."[12]

It is possible that van der Werf has carried his arguments to an extreme in an effort to correct the overemphasis on the modal rhythms. After all, the few songs that do appear in a definite rhythmic notation do approach the patterns of modal rhythm. The manuscripts do give the impression that these pieces were sung in a number of different ways, and we may rightly assume that they were not performed identically by, say, a professional jongleur at a singing contest, a clerk studying at the university in Paris, or a noble lady singing them for her own amusement. Indeed, the manuscript transmission of the songs, not only the so-called trouvère manuscripts, but also the great motet collections of the 13th century, give us a hint to the kind of circumstances under which the songs were adapted, or forced if you will, into the rhythmic patterns derived from "learned" music. Namely, when the flexible and changeable melodies became popular or used in a circle of musicians who did cultivate primarily the polyphonic forms. Then they were probably sung in the same rhythmic organization as the upper voices of the motets, and in fact many were simply incorporated into the polyphonic repertory, either as tenors or as upper voices and thus sung in modal rhythms.[13] Nevertheless, there can also be no doubt that this does not represent either their most common manner of performance nor, so to speak, their normal habitat.

UITE apart from the matter of the modal rhythm and the bitter controversy it generated, Beck's introductory chapters, particularly Chapters II and III, suffered from the fact that no careful research had yet been done on the sources of medieval post-Gregorian chant (in fact, such a research was not done until decades later), and that what little research had been done was the work of liturgists and literary historians who seldom paid much attention to the music itself. Thus Beck's brief summary of the rise of tropes, sequences, proses, and liturgical drama, contains not only numerous inaccuracies of detail, but also suffers from a wrong perspective of the large-scale development of these forms and of the spread of the repertory. In this Beck held to the traditional "German" mythology that held Notker Balbulus (d. 915) and his circle at St. Gall to be the originators of the trope and the sequence, even in the face of the disclaimer that Notker himself presents in the preface to his *Liber hymnorum*, where he states that he came upon these new forms in an Antiphoner from the north French Abbey of Jumièges.[14]

Nevertheless, Beck's word does retain its usefulness, particularly as an introduction to the repertory and to some of the poetic genres used by the troubadours, and also because, together with Pierre Aubry's *Trouvères et Troubadours*,[15] it presented one of the earliest systematic views of the music of the troubadours and the trouvères that was based upon a thorough study of the sources but at the same time was written in a simple and generally accessible manner. The view of this music presented by both Beck and Aubry became the "traditional" scholarly view precisely because their work was available not only to other specialists, but to the informed student of troubadour and trouvère poetry and to the layman as well. A work such as Beck's treatise was indeed what would have been most easily available to someone like Ezra Pound when he began to take an interest in the Old Provençal poetry and its music. This, apart from any other consideration, would more than justify the inclusion of an English translation of Beck's *La Musique des Troubadours* in the present collection.

Notes

1. A second edition appeared in Paris in 1928.

2. The rhythmic modes consist of patterns of long and short notes that are repeated over and over in a manner similar to that of poetic meters. They articulate and coordinate the different melodies of the polyphonic music of the 12th and 13th centuries. In the music of the 12th century, where the singers most often sang long vocalises on a single text syllable, the modes are indicated by the grouping of the different "ligatures" (two or more notes written in a single trait). In the 13th century, where the texts of the motets are often set with one note to a syllable, or at most two or three notes to a syllable, the necessity arose of creating a notation where the shape of the note itself would convey its length. This notation, known as "mensural notation," is the direct ancestor of our modern rhythmic notation.

The note forms of mensural notation are the same used for single notes in modal notation, or indeed in the non-measured notation used for Gregorian chant at the time, but in mensural notation these shapes are given an arbitrary (now traditional) rhythmic meaning thus:

┐ long

■ breve

♦ semibreve

The most common rhythmic modes were the following six patterns:

1. L S / L
2. S L / S
3. L S S / L
4. S S L / S
5. L L L
6. S S S / S

The slash in the chart above separates the first rhythmic "foot" from the continuation of the pattern. Note that in Modes Three and Four, where all longs are of three beats, the "shorts" could have either one beat (*brevis recta*, or "correct" short) and two beats (*brevis altera*, or "the other" short). The few trouvère melodies notated in one or another of the modes, show a systematic ordering of tailed and untailed notes, but the majority shows no discernible order in their use of one or another of the note shapes.

The best modern explanation of the rhythmic modes remains that of William G. Waite, *The Rhythm of Twelfth Century Polyphony*, Yale Studies in Music History, I (New Haven, 1954, R. Westport, 1973), pp. 13–55, but see also Willi Apel, *The Notation of Polyphonic Music*, 5th ed. (Cambridge, Mass., 1953), pp. 220–223, and Carl Parrish, *The Notation of Medieval Music* (New York, 1957, R. 1978), 73–77. Parrish also gives (pp. 41–58) a useful summary of the application of modal rhythm to monophonic songs of the middle ages.

3. J. B. Beck, "Zur Aufstellung der modaler Interpretation der Troubadour Melodien," *Sammelbände der Internationalen Musikgesellschaft*, XII (1910–1911), 316–324, where Wolf's statement and Beck's reply are given.

4. The controversy, albeit muted, continued long after the death of all the principals (Aubry, 1910, Ludwig, 1931, Beck, 1943), e.g., with Jacques Chailley, "Quel est l'auteur de la "théorie modale" dite de Beck-Aubry?" *Archiv für Musikwissenschaft*, X (1953), 212–222, finding for Aubry, and Friedrich Gennrich, "Wer ist der Initiator der 'Modaltheorie?' Suum cuique," *Miscelánea en homenaje a Monseñor Higinio Anglés* (Barcelona, 1958–1961), I, 315–330, in a reply to Chailley pressing again Ludwig's claims.

5. The most extensive arguments against the generalized application of the modal theory have been put forth by Hendrik van der Werf, *The Chansons of the Troubadours and the Trouvères, a Study of the Melodies and their Relation to the Poems* (Utrecht, 1972).

6. On the beginnings of Musicology see Alfred Einstein, *Music in the Romantic era* (New York, 1947), pp. 352–355.

7. With very few exceptions, most 18th and 19th century music historians worked with whichever sources lay easily at hand. Most library collections were badly catalogued and often completely unknown or inaccessible.

8. Montpellier, Faculté de Médecine, MS. H. 196, published in a facsimile and transcription by Yvonne Rokseth, *Polyphonies du XIIIe siècle, le manuscrit H. 196 de la faculté de médecine de Montpellier*, 4 vols. (Paris, 1935–1939), Bamberg, Staatsbibliothek, MS. Lit. 115 (*olim* Ed. IV. 6), published in facsimile and transcription by Pierre Aubry, *Cent motets du XIIIe siècle, publiés d' après le manuscrit Ed. VI. 6 de Bamberg*, 3 vols. (Paris, 1908, R. New York, 1964), Paris, Bibliothèque Nationale, MS. *français* 146, fols. 1–36, published in facsimile by Pierre Aubry, *Le Roman de Fauvel, reproduction phototypique du manuscrit français 146 de la Bibliothèque Nationale de Paris . . .* (Paris, 1907), modern edition of the polyphonic pieces in Leo Schrade, *Polyphonic Music of the Fourteenth Century*, I (Monaco, 1954).

9. *Repertorium organorum recentioris et motetorum vetustissimi stili*, I. *Catalogue raisonné der Quellen 1. Handschriften in Quadratnotation* (Halle, 1910). Ludwig continued working on this to his death in 1931. Vol. I, part 2, and Vol. II were still in page-proofs at his death, but he published an abridged version of Vol. I/2 as "Die Quellen der Motetten ältesten Stils," *Archiv für Musikwissenschaft*, V (1923), 185–222, 273–315. Vols. I/2 and II were published posthumously by Friedrich Gennrich, in *Summa musicae medii aevi*, VII and VIII (Darmstadt, 1961–1962).

10. Strassburg, 1908.

11. Hendrik van der Werf, "The Trouvère Chansons as Creations of a Notationless Culture, *Current Musicology*, I (1965), 61–68, "Deklamatorische Rhythmus in der Chanson des Trouvères," *Die Musikforschung*, XX (1967), 122–144, "Concerning the Measurability of Medieval Music," *Current Musicology*, X (1970), 69–73, and *The Chansons of the Troubadours and the Trouvères* (Utrecht, 1972). Van der Werf is also engaged in a critical edition of all of the trouvère melodies, the first volume of which had been published, *Trouvères Melodien*, I: *Blondel de Nesle, Gautier de Dargies, Chastelain de Coucy, Conon de Béthune, Gace Brulé*, Monumenta monodica medii aevi, XI (Kassel, Basel, Tours, London, 1977).

12. Ernst Rohloff, ed., *Der Mensuraltraktat des Johannes de Grocheo*, Mediae latinitatis musica, II (Leipzig, 1943), also, Johannes de Grocheo, *Concerning Music (De musica)*, ed. and trans. by Albert Seay (Colorado Springs, 1967).

13. On this see Henrich Husmann, "Zur Rhythm des Trouvèregesanges," *Die Musikforschung*, V (1952), 110–131, Friedrich Gennrich, "Grundsätzliches zur Rhythmik der Mittelalterliche Monodie," *Die Musikforschung*, VII (1954), 150–176, and Friedrich Gennrich, *Lateinische Kontrafaktur, eine Auswahl Lateinische Conductus mit ihrem Volksausspachigen Vorbildern*, Musikwissenschaftliche Studienbibliothek, XI (Darmstadt, 1956), where a number of trouvère songs are compared with their polyphonic versions in an effort to determine the correct rhythm. For an extensive list of trouvère songs incorporated into polyphonic works see Nico J. H. van de Boogard, *Rondeaux et refrains du XIIe siècle au début du XIVe* (Paris, 1969).

14. Notker's preface, and a very good account of the sequence's evolution appear in Richard L. Crocker, *The Early Medieval Sequence* (Berkeley, 1977). On the tropes the most useful introduction is Paul Evans, *The Early Trope Repertory of Saint-Martial de Limoges*, Princeton Studies in Music II (Princeton, 1970).

15. 2nd ed. (Paris, 1910), trans. by Claude Avery (New York, 1914, R. 1969).

Foreword

S it is never easy to reveal the results of scientific research to readers lacking specific training, the task before me is a particularly arduous one, especially so when it concerns a subject as broad and as little examined as the music of songs composed in the vernacular language of the middle ages.

Philologists, whatever their opinions on the subject, from the least to the most respected of them, have never disputed the importance of music in the work of the Troubadours.[1] If they have not succeeded in unraveling the characteristics of this music, it is because the secret of the older, unmeasured system of notation has eluded them. Limited to song writers, their research has had too narrow a base to result in any satisfactory conclusions. Furthermore, the history of religious music is so alien to Philology that specialists in Romance languages, who interest themselves only in the lyrics of the Troubadours, have never attempted to address the subject.

For several years I have involved myself with this task, in consultation with the eminent romanist from Strasbourg, M. G. Groeber, and have been fortunate to uncover the latent rhythm present in compositions scored by means of a system of neumes or quadrangles. Moreoever, in continuing this line of investigation, we have been able to establish unequivocally the very strict relationship that exists between the melodies of the Troubadours and the religious music of the middle ages. I wrote my first work on *Die Melodien der Troubadours* to be submitted to professional musicologists for their judgements upon our methods and conclusions. It now appears beneficial to summarize our research in a more convenient edition, elementary enough so that even readers unfamiliar with the history of music will be able to form some idea about the songs of the Troubadours and the proper means to reconstruct them.

That is the intention of this book. I have had to neglect all nonessential details, no matter how interesting, in order not to confuse the reader with the abundance of material available. Also, it has not been possible to present justifiable proof for each and every position that this book affirms. Nevertheless, considering that an elementary work misses its point if instead of making a subject understandable it confines itself to the assertion of facts, I have attempted as a general rule to explicate, at least summarily, every point I shall propose.

1. Unless otherwise stated, in this book I am using the term Troubadour to indicate both troubadour and trouvère.

PART ONE

I

Troubadours and Trouvères

HE word *troubadour* evokes in the popular imagination an image of a romantic young singer, pale and wan, with a languorous expression on his face, the traditional lute or lyre in his delicate hands. The statuette of the *Florentine Singer* with its simpering affectation represents this legendary stereotype. Yet these preconceptions do an injustice to the accurate image of the troubadours and trouvères of the middle ages.

Troubadour and *Trouvère* are terms, one Provençal and the other French, which during the eleventh through the fourteenth centuries were applied to the authors of songs written in the vernacular language on both sides of the Loire river. These two terms are best translated by the word *composer* or better still *inventor*. *Trobar* (provençal) and *trover* (French) are the old forms of the French word *trouver*, to find. *Trobador* (nominative *trobaire*) and *troveor* (nominative *trovère*) designates one who *finds*, that is, one who *invents* the words and music to songs. Like certain modern composers, the authors of the songs of the middle ages were at the same time "inventors" of music (*note* in Provençal and *son* in French) and of words (*motz, mos*). This was the customary approach, however in practice there were certainly exceptions. This will become apparent as we retrace in detail the work of these ancient song writers. What should concern us at present is the degree to which these "inventors" deserve that title, not so much as individuals, but in the general, historical context. Were troubadours and trouvères really the creators of a poetry that was sung in the vernacular? To answer this question, it is first necessary to examine the literary and musical compositions which preceded the earliest products of the troubadours.

II

The Period Preceding the Troubadours

ELL before the time of Guilhem IX, count of Poitiers (1071–1127), the earliest troubadour whose works we possess, there were in France nomadic singer-musicians called *histrions, mimes* and *jongleurs*. These singers roamed the country from the north to the Midi, following the main trade routes, stopping at the castles of noble lords and at village crossroads. They established themselves at fairs and festivals (usually coinciding with religious ceremonies), performing wherever they might hope to find renumeration.

Their talents were, as might be expected, rather diverse: from acrobats who accompanied their buffoonery with notes struck upon some primitive instrument, to accomplished minstrels who alternated their love songs and historical recitations with *ritornelli* and *intermezzi* performed on the lyre, the psaltry or the harmonium. All types of entertainers must doubtless have been represented by these traveling players.

Despite the popularity they enjoyed among the people, perhaps because of it and because of the influence they exercised over the popular imagination, performing songs in the vernacular which were not always edifying but which must have been listened to with more interest than the sermons and canticles heard in Latin in the church, the clergy reacted emphatically against these forms of popular amusement.

From passages of certain decrees of religious councils we are acquainted with the measures taken by bishops opposing the introduction of the *mimes* into the divine services. A text from the sixth century (from Caesar of Arles, died 542) informs us, in a statement banishing them, of the existence of "infamous and diabolic songs of love".

For these measures to have their desired effects it was not enough to forbid subversive songs; it was necessary to replace them with something else. The more learned monks applied themselves to substituting pious canticles for the licentious creations of the *histrions*. To fill the minds of the people with subjects which would not endanger the salvation of their souls, they translated, from Latin into the vernacular, passages from the Scriptures and the more popular Lives of the Saints.

ONE monk of the ninth century, Otfried of Wisemburg, tells us rather sententiously that he replaced these immoral songs with the most beautiful passages of the Gospel which he translated into the German language. And, in order that his pious work might afford a greater audience, he turned them into rhymed verse.

In France, the same tendency resulted in the translation of the renowned Boethius and of the *Life of Sainte Foi d'Agen* (Provençal text) and of the pieces of *Sainte Eulalie, Saint Léger, The Passion* and *Saint Alexis* (French texts) and undoubtedly certain others that have not come down to us.

A manuscript from Limoges preserves fragments written in the dialect of that region, among which is a canticle in honor of the Virgin: *O Maria Deu Maire* (Hail Mary Mother of God), which has long intrigued scholars. An examination of the notation of this manuscript reveals the pleasant surprise that this enigmatic canticle is simply an adaptation of a hymn attributed to Fortunatus (sixth century)—perhaps the most popular of his hymns—the admirable *Ave Maris Stella*. Although the manuscript dates from the end of the eleventh century, we can certainly trace its composition to an earlier date, since the text we have is not in the hand of the author, but rather consists of a collection of fragments from diverse periods.

Although we possess valuable examples of religious poetry written in the vernacular during this remote time, the situation is quite different in regards to secular poetry. Since education was in the hands of the clergy and the majority of lay people could neither read nor write, this poverty of manuscript material ought not to surprise us. Out of necessity, poetry that was not religious had to be transmitted orally, therefore the absence of written materials should not lead us to conclude that secular work never existed. There can be no doubt that songs have always existed, but the question we should consider is whether the secular songs prior to those of the troubadours can be termed "literature" in the formal sense of that word.

The sudden appearance of a genre already in the highest state of formal development, is the phenomenon confronting us in the works of the first known troubadours, and one which has consistently intrigued men of letters. All works on the subject, regardless of their depth, are attempts to explain this curiosity. Certain philologists have assumed that the poetry of the troubadours had a popular origin. It is, however, difficult to see even the earliest Provençal lyrics, whose couplets achieve such technical polish, deriving in any direct way from humble folksong.

Popular compositions, whether music or words, are not necessarily deficient in grace, but their technique is certainly unaccomplished. The use of subtlety, which presupposes a certain refinement, is contrary to the rather indelicate penchant of the masses. Just as the poetic ideas expressed by the people are often simple and without variation, so their form, and by this I mean the musical sense as well as the verse form, often bears witness to a dreadful poverty of imagination and workmanship.

To maintain that the songs of the troubadours, so subtle and so complex from their beginnings (Guilhem of Poitier, Cercamon, Marcabru), works by men who made it a point of honor "to compose impenetrably" (*trobar clus*), are derived from popular songs is to say only that both are composed of words sung in the vernacular language. This explains nothing. It does not resolve the problem; it ignores it entirely.

When only the text of the songs is being studied, the origins of troubadour poetry must remain open to mystery. As a literary phenomenon, the work of the troubadours is unique. No matter how erudite a philologist may be, he will search in vain among the vast treasure of early literary works for songs possessing, even remotely, the characteristics of troubadour poetry. The study of this subject should be reserved not for the history of literature, but for the history of music. Music, in fact, is not only integral to the work of the troubadours, but to a large degree determines what poetic form a song takes.

Furthermore, it is easier and more definite to study the musical origin of these songs than their poetic origins; since the musical expression of a sentiment is more vague than its poetic expression, genres of music are consequently less varied than genres of poetry. For example, the exultant emotion of love is the foundation for many different emotions: religious passion, filial devotion, patriotism, physical desire, etc., all of them nuances of the same sentiment. In poetry, each of these variations would be expressed in a different manner. This is not the case in music; a single musical phrase may express them all. For this reason it has been possible to adapt the melody of the *Tantum ergo* into the melodies of subsequent Russian and Austrian hymns. Likewise the *Romance Without Words* of Mendelssohn, and other secular songs, borrow their melodies from the musical text of the *O Salutaris*. The *Ave Maria* was composed from a tune in Field's *Nocturne* and from a hundred other melodies borrowed from contemporary operas.

Though it is difficult to find true relationships between the poetry of the troubadours and the poetry that preceded it, it is possible, *a priori*, to expect that a study of the music may lead more readily to the origins of this genre. For, instead of tracing the unique similarities between troubadour poetry and its predecessors, we have the opportunity of recovering the musical sources through an extensive investigation of the entire storehouse of music preceding the appearance of the first troubadour.

Indeed, while recently studying the religious music of the middle ages, I was compelled to remark, as I had anticipated I would, the strict relationship that existed therein with the tunes of secular songs. The music of the tenth and eleventh centuries is so obscure that I feel it is important to say something about it at this point.

Ancient Christianity incorporated, in addition to the ritualistic canticles and other divine offices of the mass still extant today in the *plain song*, certain other pieces which have since disappeared from the lay mass. Among these were abundant vocalizations of *Alleluia*, called *sequelae*, which sometimes lasted for a duration of a thousand notes demanding singers specially trained for this rigorous exercise in harmony. Neglecting, for the moment, compositions sung directly from prose texts (*Antiphone, Responsus, Kyrie, Gloria, Offertorium*, etc.), we should mention the hymns of this period which from their inception followed the rules of Latin prosody and were strictly poetic texts (hymni metrici). Later, rhythmic hymns (hymni rhythmici) were composed, where on the contrary, it was music which dominated the verse. These were composed of a certain number of syllables assembled in such a manner that, in principle, a correlation might exist between the tonic accent of the words and the rhythmic accent or accented beat of the music.

Toward the end of the ninth century an important innovation took place at the celebrated abbey of Saint-Gall in Switzerland. Notker (died 912) and his pupils, Radpert, Tutilon, and Hartmann, adapted poetic texts to the *Alleluia*. Instead of the older technique of vocalizing on the vowels of the word *Alleluia*, they began to sing a series of words, relating one syllable of text to each note of the primitive *Alleluia*. These new compositions were called *prosae* and *sequentiae*. The stanzas of these hymns were usually composed of four to six verses, often linked by assonance (the homophony of the last tonic vowel of the verse, and sometimes of all the vowels which coincide with the accented beat). In rhymed *sequentiae* the stanzas were joined two by two.

To these compositions based on the principle of the repetition of a musical phrase are attached the notion of Tropes, which are transformations and interpolations of traditional liturgical chants (formally established in the sixth century by Saint Gregory) such as the *Introitus*, the *Kyrie*, the *Gloria*, etc. These Tropes consist of the repetition of each phrase or musical concept inserted into a new text, composed *ad lisitum*. In the tropes of the *Kyrie*, as in the *sequentiae* of the *Alleluia*, the liturgical melody is preserved, while in other tropes poetic and musical interpolations are added from other pieces. Quite naturally, at the outset the authors of these hymns, tropes and prosae concerned themselves more with the expression of their profound religious sentiments rather than with the perfection of their poetic technique. Their efforts toward a powerful poetic expression did not exclude a certain vagueness. Religious exaltation is often mystical and therefore not necessarily lucid. Poets of this period were consumed by powerful sentiments, but they were not yet capable of analysing and translating these feelings with much precision. This explains the substantial role which convention plays in their poetry. The same terms, the same epithets and the same images recur repeatedly in the tropes and prosae. These clichés are used as conventional formulae for the expression of individual experience which could not be rendered by other means.

The musical portion of these compositions is more firmly grounded. This is easy to understand if one recognizes that in music the analysis of sentiment is unnecessary but that music defines itself by expressing emotions through an association with auditory impulses.

OTKER and his school exercised a profound influence on religious music. The abbeys at Reichenau (by Lake Constance) and Murbach (near Guebwiller in Alsace), just to name two of the dependencies of Saint-Gall, have handed down to us precious manuscripts generally contemporary with Notker. Their movement soon gained a prominence over the whole of France, reaching a particularly high degree of development in Limousin. One fact that has been overlooked, but which in fact dominates the musical history of this epoch, is that the abbey of Saint-Martial of Limoges, alone, has bequeathed us twenty manuscripts, forming a veritable *corpus* of liturgical hymns, tropes and prosae from the tenth through the thirteenth centuries. Twenty manuscripts, though it may not seem much to the reader unfamiliar with the extant Medieval library, is an enormous collection. It would be an important find for the history of literary manuscripts; it is prodigious as concerns the history of music.

If one considers that the first troubadours, and likewise the best, originated from regions bordering Limousin and that the literary language in which they wrote, regardless of their origins, was called by contemporaries *lengua lemosina*, it would be foolish to consider this a mere coincidence. Monastic schools required, during the middle ages, the teaching of music in their curriculum for advanced studies (quadrivium). This instruction, both practical and theoretical, was highly developed, to the degree that talented students often became accomplished musicians and composers.

URTHERMORE, as these schools were not only attended by future clerics, but also by young nobles, it is natural to suppose that the instruction in the abbeys of Limousin (Saint-Martial, Saint-Leonard and others) exercised a powerful influence over secular music. This supposition is fortified by the fact that most ancient musical compositions of the troubadours are religiously inspired. The only song of Guilhem of Poitiers in which the music has been preserved (Guilhem was a notoriously irregilious troubadour) is composed in the style of a hymn (*Pus de chantar m'es pres talens*) to such a degree that the same music can be found in a religious drama, *The Mystery of Saint Agnes*. The songs of Marcabru bear witness, with the exception of one pastoral, to the same musical influence, as also do the songs of Jaufre Rudel, Pierre d'Auvergne, the poetess, Beatrice de Die, Bernart de Ventadour and those of the majority of troubadours up to and including the last, Guiraut Riquier (1254–1292).

The biography of Gosbert de Puycibot, a troubadour of the early thriteenth century, tells us that he learned his art at the Limousin abbey of Saint-Leonard where he had been placed from early childhood to prepare for the contemplative life. The biographies of certain other troubadours contain references to their monastic education. It is my firm conviction that the more one studies the religious music of the middle ages, the more one will observe the strict relationship which exists between the melodies of religious hymns and *Alleluias*, on the one hand, and the songs of the troubadours on the other.

III

Musical Notation in the Middle Ages

A. The Transformation of Neumes

ELIGIOUS music of the middle ages, to this day, still presents many obscurities; their system of musical notation has become a major source of debate. Through the conservation efforts of modern scholars a number of interesting texts have been brought to light, but, despite the aid of these contemporary theoretical treatises on the decipherment of Medieval notation, there is still no general agreement about the value and the actual significance of the various systems. In fact, the most ancient system of notation, that of the neume, is so enigmatic that it has resisted to this day all attempts at scholarly interpretation. Nevertheless, I believe that by utilizing a comparative method which in an earlier work enabled me to penetrate the secret of the music of the troubadours, I shall be able to perform the same service here. This I shall attempt after a few words on the historical development of musical notation.

It is known that Charlemagne (768–814) received from Italy a taste for art and classical literature. His biographer, Eginhard, and other chroniclers report that he surrounded himself with the most illustrious men of his times. Numerous schools were established in the principal centers of his empire, where music, being associated with *belles-lettres*, was given a preeminent role in the artistic movement founded by the great emperor. With an eye toward the unification of liturgical music, Charlemagne prescribed the rites of the Roman Church in all the provinces of the Occident and asked Pope Adrian II to send him qualified music teachers to institute instruction in this subject. Two of the best musicians in Rome, Peter and Roman, left for Aix-la-Chapelle. The former settled in Metz, where he founded a school whose influence made itself felt not only for the quality of its compositions but also for the development of the art of notation. Until the fourteenth century, this notation in the Lorraine countryside retained a particular format, designating a transition between roman or aquitanian writing and the gothic notation of the germanic countries.

The latter, Roman, who was obliged to stay at Saint-Gall, was supposed to have brought, according to tradition (recently contested), an original copy of the antiphonary of Saint Gregory, of which an authentic reproduction is preserved in the library of the monastery. This antiphonary of Saint-Gall is notated in neumes.

Neumes are conventional musical signs originating from the accents in Greek script. They show nothing more than the direction of melodic flow, without indicating actual intervals. The two elements that constitute this system of notation are the *punctus*, period or grave accent which designates the descending movement of the voice, and the *virga*, the vertical or acute accent which marks the elevation of tone. If the two signs are combined, a configuration is obtained which indicates groupings of notes. The combination of the *punctus* and the *virga*, at the base from the left yields a sign called the *podatus*, which indicates an ascending interval. Conversely, the *clivis* formed from a punctus joining a virga to its right represents the descending direction of a group of notes, i.e., one of the possible intervals of a descending scale:

To make this clearer, let us compare analytically a particular musical phrase that appears in several manuscripts from the tenth through the twelfth centuries, the trope from the *Gloria: Laus tua Deus*, which is preserved in a series of manuscripts belonging to different regions and different periods (plate I).

Let us look at the first line of this trope, according to the most ancient version from a tropary at Saint-Gall:

Laus tua deus resonet coram te rex .(St.-Gall 484)

Here we see the *punctus* (elongated period) on the syllables, **tu**a and **re**sonet, the *podatus* (ascending interval) on the syllables, t**ua**, res**o**net and c**o**ram, here in its so called liquid form (*epiphonus*), which usually occurs at the juncture of two consonants or two semi-vowels; on the first syllable, **laus**, where it is fitted with a small hook called *episeme*, derived from a prosodic symbol for brevity. This *clivis episematica* is moreover followed by a secondary symbol in the form of an *S* called *oriscus*. This one sees replaced by another figure in other manuscripts, a figure called the *pressus* (see plate I lines V to XIII). Both refer to the prolongation of a note. Above the next to last syllable, **te**, one sees the same *clivis* just noted above the syllable **laus**. But here it is followed by a major *pressus*, and two descending notes. Above the last syllable one sees four symbols, a *virga* and three apostrophes, *strophici*, which together form a *tristropha*. Please note also the symbol called *quilisma*, which occurs after the punctus in the first syllable of **co**ram and represents an ornament similar to our present day mordant.

To make this system of notation more effective, a system of sigils were joined to the basic neumes. In this way, *e* represents the word *equaliter* so that the singer is forewarned that the following note is of equal duration to the one previous. An *i* or more simply a dot under a neume signifies *inferius*, a lower note. The explication of these symbols, attributed to Roman is revealed to us from the correspondence of Notker.

Despite the information which they furnish, these letters or sigils are not fit to reconstruct an entire song. It was only in the eleventh century that musicians succeeded in filling the most perceptible gaps in neumatic notation. Many methods were advocated at the same time. A monk from Reichenau who had attended the school at Saint-Gall, Hermann, known as *Contractus*, thought of a very ingenious system. He designated all the intervals on a scale by means of the first initial of their names. The initial *t* in *tonus* represented the major second. The *s* in *semitonium* represented a half tone, *ts* one tone plus a semitone or a minor third, *tt* two tones or a major third, etc. In this way, the melodic movement outlined by the neumes was expressed exactly and the singer was more prepared than previously when faced with an unknown song.

Italians followed another system of dictation called *diastematic*. In order to reproduce the rising and falling inflexions of the voice in their written music, they depicted melody linearly. Thus when the voice rose, the neume was placed higher than the one preceding it, and *vice versa* when the interval descended. The exterior form of the neumes became so negligible that, inevitably, the varied shapes that had been employed in the nineth century were reduced to mere points. A line traced in dry point or in red ink served as a basis for the placement of notes at distances proportional to the appropriate musical interval.

To this line a second was joined, traced in yellow ink. In order to clarify with more precision the gradation of notes within these two extremes, an intermediary line was added and above each note, the name of the note was recorded. The first bore the letter *f* (fa), the second, *a* (la) and the third *c* (do). Finally, to complete the process, lines were added to indicate the contour of the melody. Likewise, the key-letters varied according to the pitch. They gave rise to all possible combinations:

		c (do)	*a* (la)			
a (la)	*c* (do)	*a* (la)	F (fa)	F (fa)	*g* (sol)	etc.
F (fa)	F (fa)	F (fa)	*d* (ré)	*b* (si ♭)	*c* (do)	

Thanks to this invention and to the diastematic staff, musical notation became clearer. It reproduced with exactitude the form of a melody. Keep in mind too that the invention of the four lined staff is attributed to Guido d'Arezzo (first half of the eleventh century).

From the eleventh century on, certain musical notators began to add to the neumes of old manuscripts, which had become less and less intelligible, the usual designation of the notes, *cdefga(b)hc*. This combination of letters indicates the absolute span of a melody, but even this practice was quickly abandoned.

Of all the systems designed during this period, the one invented by Guy of Aretin is the only one that was viable enough to last until our time. By the twelfth century, the phrase that we have analyzed previously reappears in a manuscript from Saint-Yrieix, in the following form (we have substituted the dry point of the manuscript with a dotted line):

The neumes are wider. What were dots have become squares. They have lost their earlier significance, which has become useless because of the expedient of the *diastema*, i.e.— because of the graphic imitation of melodic movement.

The problems of interpretation that were faced in the reading of earlier neumes vanish with the invention of this system of quadrangular notation. As always, necessity stimulated the improvement. In so far as music remained monodic or diaphonic[1] there were only a few teachers who, to assist their memory, felt the need to put into writing the repertoire which they expected their students to master.

1. *Diaphonic* refers to the first attempts at songs for two voices, by means of parallel sounds, fifths, fourths and octaves.

When the invention of counterpoint or descant (*discantus*) propagated a taste for polyphonic compositions, in the technical sense of the word, choir-schools were established and it became necessary for musical notation to be read with greater ease. Quadrangular notation responded suitably to these needs. Though no longer the case for the modern reader, such notation must have been perfectly clear to readers of those days.

As has been seen, except for the neumes themselves, quadrangular notation gives no precise indication of rhythm or tempo. Contemporary musicians could, perhaps, do without the information, for they would certainly be familiar with the tempo of songs from having heard them performed. The *episeme*, the *pressus* and other symbols would eventually compensate for any weakness of memory. We shall see later (chapter IV) how it is possible today to determine this latent rhythm through a critical reading of the text alone. Plate I, which presents various reproductions[1] of the phrase analyzed above, from numerous manuscripts of the nineth through the fourteenth centuries, illustrates the successive transformations of musical writing during this first great period of its evolution.

The first four lines show the earliest neumatic notation. Naturally, the shape of the neumes varies from era to era, from place to place and even from copyist to copyist. The neumes from Saint-Gall have their distinctive character, as do those from Limousin and Aquitaine.

The notation in lines V and VI preceded the year 1031, the date of the council of Limoges when the apostolate of Saint Martial was proclaimed.

The next lines, VII through XIV, in which the *diastema* is clearly revealed, belong to the end of the eleventh and to the twelfth century. The same compositions could be cited in two additional manuscripts, one from Montoriol and the other from Arles.[2] When they were originally notated, the songs of the first troubadours could not have been recorded in any other system.

The writing in line XV is from a manuscript at Saint-Yrieix and was used from the twelfth through the beginning of the thirteenth centuries.

Line XVI is a definitive specimen of quadrangular notation, used by the Italians from the thirteenth century on. It is in this form that thousands of troubadour songs have been transmitted to us. These we shall study in the chapters to come.

---

1. Please keep in mind that the vertical dots are not in the manuscript but have been added by the author the more clearly to separate notes belonging to each word in order to facilitate the comparative analysis of these notations.
2. This tropary has been overlooked by L. Gautier.

B. Musical Notation in the Troubadour Manuscripts

LYRICAL works of the troubadours are preserved in approximately fifty manuscripts from the thirteenth and fourteenth centuries which are today deposited in the major libraries of Europe. More than half of these collections contain poetry alone without accompanying notation. It is quite possible that the music had already been lost at the time of transcription.

The songs with musical notation are dispersed among twenty song books compiled at the end of the thirteenth century. The manuscripts vary greatly in format, design and origin. Some are richly illuminated and executed with superb taste. This indicates that the manuscripts were commissioned from master calligraphers by lords who were themselves amateur musicians or collectors of books. The modest, impromptu appearance of others seems to suggest quite the opposite, that they were created for the use of less fortunate jongleurs and trouvères as *vade mecums*.

The number of songs contained in a collection varies from one hundred to a thousand or more. In most cases the poems are catalogued by the names of the authors, in several instances by literary genre, and only once by alphabetical order. M. G. Groeber has shown that the extant manuscripts are anthologies compiled from the working notebooks of individual troubadours.

The manuscripts destined for notation were from the outset arranged in such a way that the scribe in charge of copying the text would first draw in a musical staff or leave an open space between the lines of the first verse of each song. The notator, often a professional, would then fill these in. There are also in the possession of libraries manuscripts in which both the text and music are transcribed by the same hand. It is quite exceptional to find cases where the music is repeated in the second verse.

The staves range from two to eight lines, according to the requirements of the melody and the space available. Those which are four to five lines, traced in red ink, occur most frequently. The clefs of *fa* or *ut* are placed at the head (front) of the staff in such a way that the notes do not extend beyond the lines.

Sometimes the end of a musical phrase (*distinctio*) is denoted by a vertical bar resembling the measure bars in modern notation.[1] Contrary to the opinions of several scholars, these bars have no musical importance, often they are omitted entirely. Occasionally they serve the sole purpose of separating notes from words to which they do not belong.

The symbol for chromatic changes are the flat (*b molle*) before *si*, rarely before *mi*, and the natural (*b quadratum*). The flat lowers the note before which it is placed by a half tone and the natural raises it. This latter symbol fulfilled the function of the modern *sharp*. A symbol representing our modern *natural* does not exist in the extant manuscripts. In order to return a note to its natural state when under the influence of a chromatic, it was simply a matter of employing the opposite symbol.

1. Let us remember in passing that the regular use of measures does not precede the seventeenth century.

MUSICAL notes, as we have seen, are enlarged neumes, transformed to the quadrangular. The period is changed into a square, the *virga* into a square with a descending tail on the right. When several notes are to be sung on a single syllable they are grouped or linked together and are called conjunctures or ligatures.

It has long been maintained that the symbols of this ancient system of notation graphically signal the measure, the duration of the specific sound. This system was originally proposed by E. De Coussemaker (1803–1876), the learned historian of music.

The examination of a song in which one unit of a phrase is notated a second time should have sufficed to show that the notes do not possess an absolute value since, in corresponding position, they often differ in appearance. When the same song is notated in several manuscripts, the different versions should agree if the notes were expressing values of duration, yet this absolute agreement never occurs.

These differences in the notations of the same musical text do not only invalidate the system of De Coussemaker and his adepts, but may inversely indicate a solution to the problem.

Let us take for example the first musical phrase from a song honoring the Virgin, in the form of a *sequentia* taken from the manuscript of Saint Yrieix whose notation has already been examined in plate I line XV.

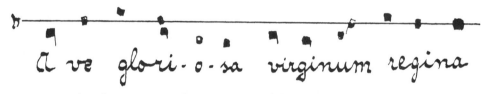

These are oversized neumes, diastematized by means of a line which in this case indicates a clef on the dominant *si* natural (infrequently used) and are characteristic of the dorian mode when it has been transposed.

In more sophisticated uses of quadrangular notation, the same melody recurs in a number of song-books from the thirteenth century, either with the same Latin text, in a French version, or in a secular text as in the *Lai des Hermins* and the *Lai de la Pastourelle*. Here below then, according to five different manuscripts, are these six reproductions set side by side:

It would be senseless to look for rhythmic indications in these manuscripts; all the notes are uniform and there is no possible way to determine their division into measures. Should we then believe that these verses were sung with regularity and simplicity of rhythm since the notation does not express the measures?

To answer this question, let us examine yet two other manuscripts, one from Soissons and the other from the British Museum in London. In the former, the musical notation appears to be proportional, which as the word implies, expresses by means of special symbols the different relationships existing in the duration of notes.

Notice the regular alternation between longs (♩) and shorts (■), especially when there is only one note on each syllable of text. On the syllables, glo**ri**osa and vir**gi**num, we see ligatures or groups of two notes.

In the London manuscript, the melody was first written in quadrangular notation. Then, towards the beginning of the fourteenth century, a copyist who was *au courant* with the new method of notation called franconian (after the inventor, Francon of Cologne, middle of the thirteenth century) transformed it by means of erasure and retouching.

Here we see the longs (⌐) from the Soissons copy replaced by shorts (▪) and these in turn by diamond shapes representing quarter notes (semibreves). The values are therefore reduced by a half, as in reducing ¾ to ⅜.

Since the manuscript from London, which reduces by a half the longs from the Soissons manuscript, is also obliged to reduce the shorts in the same way, it must be concluded that this *sequentia* is sung in measure with notes of different durations alternating symetrically.

The examination of melodies preserved in other scripts verifies these observations. The conclusion one reaches from this study, of which a more complete exposition may be found in my *Die Melodien der Troubadours*, is that the efforts of notators from Saint Gregory (sixth century), Roman (nineth century), Guido d'Arezzo (eleventh century), Francon of Cologne (thirteenth century), Phillip of Vitry (fourteenth century), up to the theoreticians and composers of recent times, in fact, until Wagner, have always worked toward the same end: *to make music notation more and more clear, obliging it to reproduce in a system of writing, as faithfully as possible, the thought of a composer.* What is of concern is not the nature of sound but the means of recording it.

One can easily conceive of a melody notated by means of an infinite number of systems since any system is a convention, without which the rhythmic quality or the meaning of the melody would not necessarily experience any change. In any case, when, among the several extant copies of the same song, we find a more precise system of notation than another, that is the one that is chosen. Therefore, one may conclude that *the rhythm indicated by this notation is equal to those indicated by all the other notations, even when only a hint of rhythm exists.* Exception is made for certain genres of polyphonic music where special reasons may cause the rhythm of a text to vary.

This principle, taken from a comparative study of manuscripts notated during the nineth through the fourteenth centuries, is confirmed by the collection of theoretical works from the same period which deal with musical notation. They inform us, in effect, how the variety of systems of notation could result in a singer being quite capable of reading the notes to his own manuscript, and yet, being incapable of deciphering those in the text of a fellow musician.

Numerous variations are found in the sequentia, *Ave Gloriosa*, sometimes written in quadrangular notation, sometimes in proportional notation. The majority of songs, however, are known in their first form, which does not indicate the rhythm. Nevertheless, we can determine it by researching the theoretical principles upon which the art of measurement and rhythm in the middle ages are based.

All verse, even that not written for song, possesses a rhythm. It is this quality which distinguishes poetry from prose. Versification obviously varies according to country and period. The rhythm of romantic French poetry, for example, differs from, not only modern German poetry, but likewise from the French poetry of the middle ages. The study of these different systems is the province of philologists. Philology, however, also differs in regards to location and levels of development. There are languages in which the rules of versification are insufficiently understood; the prosody of old Provençal and old French still requires clarification. Nevertheless, philology has succeeded in establishing the essential rules which may eventually help to resolve the problems which confront us today.

To accomplish this, it will be necessary to establish which musical principle corresponds to which rhythmic principle in the study of versification. The correlation between poetic rhythm and musical rhythm presumes, without a doubt, that these songs were poems to be sung. In performing a song, it is possible only to apply one rhythm at a time. Should there be a divergence between the rhythm of the poem and that of the melody, one or the other must be sacrificed. One does come across compositions in which both words and music express equal discord, but that is a subject to return to later and one that is certainly not of regular occurance. The troubadour who sells short the principles that regulate his art form, permits himself the euphamistic luxury of license.[1]

IV

Rhythm in the Works of the Troubadours

A. Fundamental Principles of Medieval Rhythm

ISTINCTIO or a musical phrase is composed, as is known, of a certain number of notes arranged in measures (the *perfectiones* of medieval theorists). Each measure consists of a set number of units or elements which can be arranged in a series and still have the same total value (*aequipollentia*). The first element of each measure is known as the accented or down beat; the other beats are ordinarily unaccented. These designations, accented and unaccented, indicate in themselves a difference in intensity. One can see this clearly by either singing or listening to any phrase of a song. Let us take as an example the following Christmas song:

Deck the/halls with/boughs and/holly*

1. The method that I have used in this chapter to establish the principles of medieval notation and which I discovered as early as 1905, was presented in publication for the first time in 1907 by M. Pierre Aubry, in an article in the *Revue Musicale*, vol. XII, p. 352 ss., without mentioning my name, although the documentation of M. Aubry's arguments rested on information that I had revealed and whose content, which was of a strictly confidential nature, seemed protected by his promise to keep to himself my discovery. My article in the Strasbourg journal, Caecilia (July 1907, p. 97 f.), being a precise exposition, is the first original statement of my theory of the interpretation of modes. It is developed in detail in my *Die Melodien der Troubadours*, Strasbourg, 1908 (Trubner, ed.).

*Translator's note—As M. Beck's example does not properly scan in English translation, I have provided this verse as an alternate.

The first beat of each measure (deck, halls, boughs, hol-) are sung more emphatically than the unaccented (the, with, and, -ly). The singer pronounces the former with more force, and the listener hears this difference in accent. Furthermore, an unaccented beat may fall indiscriminately on either a long or a short note.

Spoken language too is subject to the alternating rhythm of accented and unaccented beats. According to the intensity with which the lungs expel air, the vibrations of which produce sounds, variously accented vowels occur, called by philologists, tonic and atonic. In the following phrase, *you and I are here to stay, I, here* and *stay* receive greater accentuation than the other words. Though still perceptible, the variance in intensity with which these words are pronounced may not be as marked in our modern language as it certainly was in old Provençal and old French, albeit never attaining the same degree of accentuation as that in the Germanic languages.

It is clear that, in a sung text, the accented beats correspond to the tonic syllables of the verse. Discord between the down beat and the tonic accent is unpleasant to the ear. This disagreeable result may be avoided by prolonging, to the detriment of the note placed under the accented beat, the duration of a note corresponding to a tonic syllable which is to be sung on an unaccented beat.

An example should demonstrate this technique. In the line, *Robert, veez de Perron,* neglecting for the moment the rhyming syllable, the syllables *-bert* and *-ez* contain the tonic accent, while the other are atonic. If one sang in the following rhythm

Robert veez de Perron

an unpleasant sensation might result, but if one took the trouble to sing, in the manner of Thibaut of Champagne:

there is no offense. On the contrary, the flow of language, to which our ear is no longer accustomed, becomes surprisingly agreeable.[1]

1. This rhythm is often found in Hungarian music and Basque songs.

The last tonic syllable of a line is the one which receives the strongest accent. All rhymed verse demands that the syllables which rhyme be pronounced with particular intensity, so that the ear may perceive the homophony. It is for this reason that the rhymed syllable must always be placed on an accented beat. In monodic songs, this rule allows for no exceptions. Every troubadour observes it strictly, because to disobey it is more than poetic license, it is a grave error.

The last measure is reserved for the syllable or syllables of a rhyme. When the rhyme is masculine, i.e., when the line ends on a tonic syllable, as for example *Perron*, this last syllable, *ron*, occupies the first part of the last measure which is completed by a rest.

When, on the contrary, the rhyme is feminine, i.e., when the accented syllable of a rhyme is followed by an atonic syllable, as for example:

Quand li/rossi-/gnols s'es-/crie,

the attonic syllable shares its duration with the tonic, unless it is not to be prolonged, as often happens in verses of less than seven syllables, when the author wishes to produce a musical phrase of four measures.

Another principle of rhythm in the middle ages is that of regularity. An examination of the songs that are preserved in measured notation reveals to us that in the majority of cases, the rhythm established in the first measure continues for an entire phrase, sometimes even for the whole song.

This deduction is confirmed by theoretical treatises of the middle ages. One author from the thirteenth century says that "in all rhythms regularity must be observed" (*in omnibus modis ordo debet servari*).

Let us enumerate some general rules:
1. There is a correlation between tonic accents in words and accent in music.
2. The duration is increased when an accented syllable coincides with an unaccented beat and the unaccented syllable coincides with an accented beat.
3. It is impossible to place a rhyme anywhere other than on an accented beat.
4. Ordinarily, rhythm is regular.

These are the fundamental principles of troubadour rhythm. They allow us to understand and to explain the diverse rhythms of the musical works of the middle ages up to the fourteenth century.

B. Time in Medieval Composition

HE system of musical measurement in the middle ages is based on the theory of modes (*modus*).

Modes are rhythmic formulas which demote two principle groupings: those of two elements and those of three elements.

Modes of two elements consist of one long, having a value of two units, followed or preceded by one short which has a value of one. In the first mode, the long is found only at the beginning of a measure, on the accented beat. In the second, on the contrary, the short is placed on the beat.

In the first, the alternation of long and short corresponds to the following rhythm:

¾ ♩♪|♩♪|♩♪|♩♪| or by reduction, ⅜ or ⁶⁄₈ ♪♪|♪♪|♪♪|♪ |

The second mode is configured in modern notation in the following manner:

¾ ♪♩|♪♩|♪♩|♪♪♪| with the accent on the quarter note in each measure.

The third mode has three elements. The first is a long of three units duration. The second is a short of one unit and the third is a short called *altera* which has a value of two units. This mode corresponds to ⁶⁄₄ 𝅗𝅥.♩♩| or, by reduction, ⁶⁄₈ ♩.♪♩| in modern notation.

In addition to these principle modes, polyphonic art employed secondary modes, formed by the subdivision or contraction of elements constituting the three modes mentioned above.[1]

It is not absolutely necessary that a musical phrase begin on the first beat of a measure. An up beat can precede the first accent (*anacrusis*). For example, in the "Arlesienne" one sings, *Al-/lume/ton flam-/beau ver-/meil* ♪|♪♪|♪♪|♪♪|♪ | and in old French one sings, *Je/doi bien/estre o-/beis-/sant,* and in old Provençal, *tuit/cil qui/sont en-/amou-/rat.*

---

1. It is not possible to distinguish the modes except by a system of ternary subdivision. Actually, until the beginning of the fourteenth century, the middle ages knew only of the ternary subdivision. At this period then, counting in "two" and binary division were introduced. Ternary modes composed of two elements |♩♪|♩♪||, ♪♩|♪♪♪|| and |𝅗𝅥. 𝅗𝅥.|𝅗𝅥. ▬·| blended into a middle form |♩♪♪|♪♪| representing the compromise between the first and second modes of the ancients. The third mode became in its binary form |𝅗𝅥♪♪|♩♪♪| or |♪♪♪♪|♩♪|, etc.

ET, as in modern music, one can include this unaccented beat in the first measure by allowing it to share time equally with the beats that follow it. In the "Arlesienne",

/O grand so-/leil

serves as a parallel to,

/Puisque d'a-/mer

This is an infraction upon the regularity of rhythm since the first measure of a phrase sung in the first mode allows for only two elements, and here we see three. However, this infraction is justifiable. In the first and second mode, this *anacrusis* only occurs in verses of equal numbers of syllables. The most common occurence of this type in ancient lyric poetry is in verses of eight syllables. On the other hand, the most frequently encountered verses of unequal syllables contain seven syllables and begin on the down beat in order to end again, after an alternation of accented and unaccented syllables, on the down beat. Analogously, eight syllable and other verses containing an equal number of syllables begin in a like manner, especially when the anacrustic syllable is longer or more heavily accented than what follows. For example:

Puisque d'a-/mer   sounds better than   Puis-/que d'a-/mer.

Since the music must preserve its triplicity, the long (the first element of the first mode) shares time with the half note that follows, becomes by necessity .

The decomposition of an element in a group of notes of equal length is perfectly acceptable and is encountered frequently. It is evident that long notes benefit the most from this kind of division, because, in modes of two elements, the presence of a ligature on the accented beat indicates, in principle, the first mode, likewise a group of notes on the unaccented beat is more characteristic of the second mode. It is also the case that the short is resolved in even smaller values of time, especially so when its resolution is used ornamentally.

In the first mode , the weight of the rhythm is concentrated on the first element, whose intensity and duration denotes a very clear opposition to the second element. This strongly cadenced rhythm is particularly fitting in Germanic languages, where the differences in degree of intensity and duration of sound form pronounced contrasts between tonic and atonic syllables. The flow of the French and the Provençal languages is more uniform. Contrast between long and short syllables, diminished in importance today, could not have been much more important in the middle ages. In studying texts in which the notation indicates differences of duration, one sees that a word such as *amour* corresponds equally well, musically, to , as to or This indicates that the two syllables are not so dissimilar. Likewise, the difference in accentuation between the tonic and atonic is not as pronounced as in Germanic languages.

It is for this reason that a phrase constructed in the first mode will not produce a disagreeable result, in either French or Provençal, if sung in the second mode. In fact, the second mode, where the relationship between the two elements is less abrupt, more equal than in the first mode, is an excellent rhythm for French and Provençal composition. In this mode, the intensity of the downbeat is counterbalanced by the duration of the unaccented beat.

The minute and droning rhythm of ¾ time | ♩ ♪ | is admirably suited to the steady movement of Romance languages.[1]

Any measure composed of two elements in the second mode can be sung in French or Provençal. The first mode is acceptable only when the tonic accent coincides with the accented beat of the measure. These are the conclusions reached by a study of the natural rhythm of these two languages.

Those manuscripts in which the notation marks the rhythm by distinguishing long and shorts (modal notation) are clarified by treatises on the theory of modes written by contemporary theoreticians; further, they instruct us in the rhythmic formulas employed in vernacular songs. These same sources indicate a fifth rule for medieval rhythm which can be added to the four we have already formulated:

5. In a song, only one syllable relates to each element in a mode.

Therefore, in modes of two elements, there may be or should be only two syllables in each measure, and three syllables in modes of three elements.

These conclusions concerning the study of songs are supported by a notation which graphically indicates the rhythm. Is it possible to apply these conclusions to songs written in quadrangular script, where the eye does not discern a difference of duration? The reader should know the answer; he has seen in the preceding chapter that musical script has nothing to do with rhythm. It is mere chance that has preserved one song from the twelfth century in proportional notation, another in primitive quadrangular notation, and yet another in both forms. It would be unreasonable to suppose that the songs in quadrangular notation, in which the rhythm is not expressed, should be any different rhythmically from what one might encounter in proportional or franconian notation.

Having expressed this principle, let us proceed to reconstruct the latent rhythm in texts of unmeasured notation.

---

1. In the rhythm of the second mode, differences of intensity disappear; the song is allowed to flow. In this particular mode one finds the rhythm of the true *cantus planus*, a plain chant in the correct sense of the word. This is a new theory, presented here for the first time, and which shall subsequently be developed.

C. A Modal Interpretation of the Songs
of the Troubadours and Trouvères

ET us examine a sing ordinarily written in quadrangular notation:

In this uniform notation, there is nothing to indicate the duration of notes or the tempo. Therefore we must submit it to the rules we have previously formulated.

According to rule number 3, the accented syllable of a rhyme must always fall on the down beat. In our example, the rhyme occurs on the word *voie*. Therefore, we shall place a bar before this word:

Car me conseillez, Jehan, se Dex vous/voie.

If, examining the syllable preceding the rhyme, we read the line naturally, we observe the accents:

CAR me CON seilLEZ, JeHAN, se DEX vous/VOIE.

One tonic is separated from another by a single atonic. We must, therefore, conclude that the mode contains two elements and not three, since the third mode demands that two atonics succeed each tonic, as in the following verse:

DAme mer-/CI une/RIEN vos de-/MANT.

Therefore, in our example, we shall move backwards from where we set the bar and place our measures every two syllables.

CAR me/CON seil-/LEZ, Je-/HAN, se/DEX vous/VOIE.

Having done this, we observe that the tonic syllables of the text coincide with the down beat of each measure, from which it follows that the verse is structured according to the first mode. The presense of a ligature on the accented beat corresponding to the word, *Dex*, confirms that the accented beats are longs and, thus, that this song belongs to the first mode. It must, therefore, be transcribed into modern notation in the following manner:

Car   me   con — seil — liez, Je — han, se   diex   vous   voi ——— e

This interpretation can be confirmed by referring to songbook 846, whose unique importance has already been cited.[1] In fact, on page 32 of this songbook we find measured notation for our song, in the first mode. The half notes of our transcription correspond to the longs and have a value of two beats. The quarter notes correspond to the shorts and have a value of one beat.

If we were dealing with the second mode, certain tonic syllables would be placed on unaccented beats, and it would be necessary to compensate for the resulting discord by lengthening the duration of these notes. We would have to give the first element of each measure the value of one unit, and the second, occupying the rest of the measure, two units.

One must understand that the rules which we have just disclosed require neither absolute application nor mathematical precision. These are not inflexible laws, but rather, aesthetic principles. They are ideas, essentially elastic, which depend on the caprice of individual taste and style. A virtuoso, who is in full possession of his talent, may be free of them. If, in his opinion, a departure from convention will produce a desired effect, he remains no less faithful to his art.

It is also possible that such a departure will attract imitators, that it will become diffuse and fall into common usage. We see how a single verse or couplet, for that matter, may effect a change of style. These liberties are often to be seen in the songs of the twelfth and thirteenth centuries. This practice becomes even more common from the fourteenth century on, and finally becomes a customary element in modern music.

1. see Plate I, line 15.

Plate I

	Laus	tua	deus	resonet	coram	te	rex	
I								St. Gall 484
II								Prum
III								Echternach
IV								Autun
V								St. Martial Bibl. Nat. lat. 1084
VI								ibid. fol. 118 v
VII								St. Martial 1120
VIII								St. Martial 1121
IX								Nevers
X								Paris
XI								St. Martial 1118
XII								St. Martial 1119
XIII								ibid. fol. 113 v
XIV								St. Martial 887
XV								St. Yrieix
XVI								Quadr. notation

TRANSFORMATION OF MUSICAL NOTATION
FROM THE 10th TO THE 13th CENTURIES

PART TWO

II

Troubadour Melody

I. Principles and Methods

ERHAPS the ideal method of presenting the music of the troubadours and trouvères would be to publish everything that has come down to us. This was my aim in *Die Melodien der Troubadours*, and what in a forthcoming edition I propose to accomplish for the trouvères. When these publications are completed, perhaps another ten years, it will be possible to present a synthesis of the art of these songwriters. To present such an edition at this time, and in such a format as this, would be ill-considered.

In this section then, we are left with an alternative method, debatable from a scientific point of view, but appropriate enough for the purely practical aim which we have in mind. To give the reader a concise idea of the art of the songwriters of the twelfth and thirteenth centuries, the most efficient method will be to offer, with a few brief comments, actual specimens of songs chosen both from typical works and from masterworks. The picture of the lyric poetry of the middle ages given in these selections may be fragmentary, but the reader will derive a clearer idea of the general scope of the subject than he would from the minutiae of theoretical discussion, on the one hand, or details of romantic biography on the other.

There is one further comment to make concerning the manner in which these transcriptions should be presented to the public. Troubadour songs are pure melodies, sung solo, accompanied by the vielle (ancestor of the violin) if accompanied at all. The use of chords did not exist in this primitive art form, but harmonic accompaniment can be developed with the aid of the melodic element. As soon as melodic art becomes conscious of rhythm and tonality it encompasses the substance of harmony. Both religious and secular songs of this period contain a latent harmony. The notes that constitute perfect chords, in our modern sense, are to be found either in the tonal succession of notes or in their ornamentation.

Although our modern ear is accustomed to harmony, I have not seen fit to harmonize the texts here. It is true the book is addressed to the general public, but it is also, in its presentation of the texts, intended to have a documentary value. In order to benefit readers who not only wish to familiarize themselves with the nature of troubadour music, but who also wish to experience it in a contemporary aesthetic framework, I shall soon publish a collection of these songs with harmonic notation and translation into modern French.[1]

Translations will also be included of the songs in this book. The troubadours were poets as well as musicians, and the perfect agreement of words to music is an indication of the unity in their art. To deprive a song of one of its organic parts, whether words or music, would be to mutilate it. Since the majority of readers are unfamiliar with old French and know even less of old Provençal, it seemed to me absolutely necessary to present a translation below each example provided.

Certainly, my translation will not have the same literary merit that one might expect from an original poetic work. My wish to remain faithful to the sense of the text, without sacrificing rhythm or form, has imposed restraints beyond those one has to submit to in writing one's own poems.

Therefore, if my translations are far from adequate replacements for the originals, the reader should consider the difficulties involved in making parallel adaptations which are, at the same time, functional and conscious of rhyme and accent. For those who wish to understand and appreciate these songs in their original forms, the authentic text is printed in italics along with my own translation.[*]

II. The Lyrical Genres

TUDIES of troubadour lyrics have a long history. The first didactic works on the subject were written by contemporaries. The authors of these treatises, however, were not studying vernacular songs either as literary critics or historians. Rather, their intention was to formulate the principles which a troubadour ought to know in order to compose, and which readers should comprehend in order to appreciate the compositions. One of the oldest treatises in this genre, by Raimon Vidal of Besaudun (beginning of the thirteenth century), bears the title, "Theory of Composition" (*Las Razos de Trobar*). Another in the Catalan dialect is called, "The Science of Composing Poetry" (*Doctrina de Compondre Dictatz*). Besides these didactic works, commentaries were published whose purpose was to clarify the obscurities in the text of a song. Biographies were, likewise, dedicated to revealing the often obscure lives of the troubadours. The documentary value of these biographies is debatable. If they are frustrating for the philologist or historian, they are even more so for the musicologist who learns absolutely nothing of the musical education of the poets. From the *mélange* of anecdotes, there is little to be gleaned.

---

1. *Choix de Chansons de Troubadours* (twelfth and thirteenth centuries) published and transcribed with an accompaniment for piano or harp by J. Beck.

*Translator's note—An English translation will immediately follow that of M. Beck.

In their classification of the various lyric genres, the *Doctrina* and the other treatises of the fourteenth century, such as the "Laws of Love" (*Leys d'Amors*), deal exclusively with the poetry. But the categories of music are not those of poetry, since the same melody can be suited to a variety of literary genres.

It was therefore thought sufficient to classify songs simply as "joyful" or "sad," "frivolous" or "sombre", etc. For our part, we shall adhere to these traditional classifications, distinguishing between personal or subjective songs, and those which are narrative or dramatic.

A. Personal Songs

1. The Love Song (*CANSO*)

OVE is the private sentiment which most often finds expression in poetry. Whether sensual or ideal, the experience transports one to a state of exultation which may be discharged through the medium of spoken or sung verse. A high proportion of lyrics are love lyrics. This is especially true of the troubadours. The love song was the most highly developed song form in the vernacular language of the middle ages. It was designated by the name, *canso*, or short song.

Though the emotion of love is natural to all times and all countries, the form in which it is clothed varies according to period and locality. During the middle ages, the upper classes of the Midi, and consequently in the north of France, had a very refined attitude toward love, one which persists to the present day. This attitude was called the "theory of courtly love".

All love supposes the fascination of one who is possessed by the object of their desires. In the theory of courtly love, this domination was translated by the lover into a veritable worship of his lady. It was an idealistic worship, a bit mystical, yet possessing a great enobling virtue. In order to deserve the grace of his beloved (*guerredon*) the lover was obliged to honor her by long "service". If a lady should accept this hommage, she became the lord of the mind and the heart of her liege. Like all medieval servitude, this voluntary servitude was considered an unselfish act. The lover did not have the right to demand recompense for his worship, though certainly it was expected if deserved. The suitor was subject to the discretion of his lady. Her severe behavior could cause regrets and mild complaints, but would never be able to provoke any major reproach. That connection which united a man to his lady was what was designated in the middle ages as fidelity (*fe* in Provençal and *foi* in French). It was a spontaneous attachment, exempt from manipulation and subject to any degree of sacrifice. The smallest transgression would expose the transgressor to complete moral decay, to the most humiliating infamy.

To assume such strict duties, the lover had to be well convinced of the high moral quality of his lady. Moreover, the object of this love became the incarnation of all virtues, one might say the perfection of all virtues. A person, so marvelously endowed, must undoubtedly have inspired, in her circles, more jealousies than a woman today might expect to encounter in her surroundings. Likewise, slanderers became the enemies of the lover, and in their songs, troubadours were haunted by the anxiety caused by these hostilities. Perhaps we would be deceiving ourselves to interpret the origins of the discretion which was imposed by courtly love, a discretion which caused a poet to refer to his lady by a pseudonym (*senhal*), to a fear of these *losengiers* (plotters). I am of the opinion, along with M. Jeanroy, that this delicacy is a natural consequence of intimate feelings, rather than a peurile strategy to outwit the bad intentions of malingers or the curiosity of a husband. Curiosity is tenacious, and would not long be delayed by a *senhal*, despite how it veiled the lovers in mystery.

This opinion is confirmed by the custom of "impenetrable composition" (*trobar clus*), which was utilized by certain of the troubadours. It would be difficult to find a refinement of form as respectful or reluctant to profane a sublime emotion as this. The true feelings of a lover should be revealed solely to his beloved. She alone inspires him; it is for her that he composes. The indifferent and curious must be kept apart as unworthy to participate in the mystical sensibility which was designated by the troubadours as *joi e deport* (joy and rapture). Many would not be capable of appreciating this sentiment and others would only harm it by indiscreet glances. Only those rare *vrais amanz* (true lovers) would know the art of "obscure loving" and would be permitted to share the nature of the author's joy.

It is easy to see why this kind of love, which would be regarded by most with jealousy, attempts to express itself in an intimate and personal manner. Just as the troubadour's beloved resembles no other woman, and her lover resembles no other love, so his *canso* should resemble no other song. The emphasis of his art consisted of the composition of entirely original verses. The number of strophic forms that are to be found in the love songs is prodigious; it is surpassed only by the number of melodies to which they were sung. A troubadour could hardly be expected to express his most intimate thoughts with a borrowed tune, unless he were totally to ignore the consideration due his love. The *Doctrina de Compondre Dictatz* states, expressly, that each *canso* should have its own melody, as novel and beautiful as possible. All expression should be private, as it is these sentiments which dictate to the lover his *motz* and his *sons*.

When the celebrated Bernard de Ventadour (1145–1195) begins a song with the line, *Non es meravilha s'ieu chan Mielhs de nulh autre chantador* (it is no marvel if I sing better than any other singer), he is not guilty of a transgression of modesty. He is expressing a logical consequence of the theory of courtly love. Since he loves, as no one else can, a lady who is most beautiful and of the highest quality, it is no surprise that he should consider himself more inspired than any other singer.

The incontestible originality of these love songs should not lead one to think that they are exempt from the elements of convention. On the contrary, convention plays a large part in their composition, perhaps too large a part for our modern taste. Moreover, the theory of courtly love, like any doctrine concerning the emotions, is in itself a convention. Upon these foundations of convention, troubadours applied what could be considered ornamentation of formulas of style. We have already mentioned the theme of the slanderer (*losengier*), but likewise the spring and its renewal, the song of the nightingale and the warbling of other birds (*oisellons*) are themes which recur with obsessive regularity. Not only the fundamental ideas which by nature are uniform, but also their poetic expression, which should easily be accomplished with diversity, are often stereotyped. "In the month of May, when the days grow long," "the gentle, sweet song of the birds", "When the forest is covered with leaves and flowers", etc., are phrases which reoccur in a number of songs with exasperating regularity. The music, fortunately, escapes this fate for reasons which have been enumerated previously. One is convinced of this by studying the following song by Jaufre Rudel (twelfth century), the well known hero of the adventure of the Princess Lointaine, whose authenticity is much in dispute. Following is a transcription from the one and only manuscript in which the melody is preserved

When the nightingale in the woods/looking for love, gives and takes,/singing in his sweetest voice/beats his wings joyously./When water is clear and fields are gay,/when renewal reigns,/ love flows from deep in the heart.

Quite apart from the conventional character of the ideas expressed in this song, the phraseology is, if not simply commonplace, at least rather impersonal. The structure of the melody, on the contrary, is truly artistic. The first phrase is composed completely within the intervals of a fourth. This is characteristic of the *recitative*. The idea of the nightingale singing in the branches suggests to the composer the ornamentation on the last syllable, delightfully imitating the rhythm of the nightingale. The central concept of love takes the development of the melody in the second phrase up to the fifth, and culminates with an agreeable modulation in G major. In the reprise, the same gradation corresponds to the poetic text. In order to illustrate the beauties of nature, the clear streams, the green meadows, Jaufre returns to a primitive tonality, simple and with no harsh transitions. In order to express the rapture that spring gives birth to, he gradually moves the melody to its climax by shifting from B to E. The greatest tension occurs on the words *mi ven al cor*, preceding the change that follows with *grans iois cazer*. The *iois* is further accentuated by an ornament on the B. Then, with the idea that the joy of the poet will fall (*cazer*), the melody too falls into the lowest steps of the scale and ends strikingly on the subdominant note.

As a point of interest, it often happens that the final note does not correspond to the tonic note in which the melody is composed. When this is the case, it is wrong to consider the tonic note as the real ending and instead, as certain transcribers have done, to consider the real ending as the next to last note. When, for example, a melody is in the key of C major, and the final note is a D, this D is not the indicator of a gregorian mode, but rather of a partial finale, a transition to the next verse. It is always important to keep in mind the influence, during the middle ages, of the descant upon tonality. If one of the two or three voices were finishing on the tonic, the second would be finishing on the fifth above or below. This is the element which disturbs our ear when a composition has a "plagal" ending, i.e., when it does not end on the tonic. An "open" ending should tie together all the verses up to the end, which should then fall on the tonic.

The form of a melody usually encompasses a sixth, as it progresses regularly through the intervals of a major or minor scale, according to the key. When it is prolonged beyond these limits, it may extend up to a nineth and occasionally even up to a twelfth (for this reason the melody of our example occupies the intervals of a tenth). Chromatic changes are seldom used, except to avoid prohibited intervals, as for example the famous *diabolus in musica, fa-si*, or else in transpositions where it is necessary to preserve the melodic profile of the original. This usage of the flat and sharp in transpositions is most significant to an understanding of the true tonality of a melody, since notators during the middle ages did not always precisely indicate the melodic step. The presence of a chromatic sign in a transposition indicates changes that may have been omitted in the original text.

Even the summary analysis that we have just completed allows us better to appreciate the high artistic quality of the melody. Read the poetic text alone, which is somewhat commonplace, then sing it with the melody. The talent of the composer should be evident, as should the importance that music accords the medieval lyric.

The predominance of the melody over the words was commented upon by the thirteenth century biographer of J. Rudel, when he stated: *fetz de lieis mains bons vers ab bons sons ab paubres motz* (he composed for her, the Princess Lointaine, many fine songs with excellent melodies but inferior words).

Another song by the same troubadour, in which the word *lonh* (far) recurs regularly in the rhyme after the second and fourth lines of each stanza, is no less interesting than the prior example. Here is the first verse.

Modéré

Texte original / Version adaptée

Lan-quand li jorn son lonc en mai
E quand me sui par-titz de lai
Lorsque les jours sont longs en mai,
Et quand de là je pars et vai[s],

M'es bels douz chans d'au-zels de lonh.
Re-membram d'un a-mor de lonh.
Me plaît le chant d'oi-seaux de loin,
Je songe à un a-mour au loin.

Vau de ta-lan en-broncs e clis,
Sous mes ar-dents dé-sirs pli-ant

Si que chans ni flors d'al-bes-pis
Je marche et au-bé-pine et chant

Nom platz plus que l'in-verns ge-latz.
Me tou-chent moins qu'hiver ge-lé.

When the days are long in May,/pleasant is the song of birds from afar,/and when from there I go away,/I dream of a love who is far from me./Yielding to my ardent desires/I travel on, by hawthorn and song/touched less than by icy winter.

The introduction encompasses a fourth, his development rises to a sixth, then continues to develop according to the sense of the text. The personal stamp of the musician does not escape the critical eye. Once it has been established in a certain song, it is easily recognized in the ornamentation and arrangement of the phrases. This is a valuable critical element when the attribution of a text is in doubt.

It may be this particular song which formed the legend of Jaufre's love for the beautiful countess whom he had never seen. Nothing characterizes the spirit of courtly love so well as the question raised by these verses of such singular beauty. Is this addressed to a mortal? Could it just as easily be a pious hymn in honor of the virgin? This is the conjecture proposed by a fine connoisseur of troubadour poetry, M. C. Appel, and one which, after my musical inquiries, I tend to support. This example shows how little removed troubadour lyrics are from the hymns of the church, and how essential it is, to the history of Provençal literature, to acquire an understanding of the religiously inspired lyrics of the middle ages.

NE may observe, in the song transcribed above, the repetition of the two opening musical phrases. This repetition corresponds to the stanza structure in the poetic text, however, this correspondance is not in the least obligatory. These verses can be arranged according to the schema *aa bb ccd*, and likewise, the music can be considered as the progressive development of a single idea. When a stanza is a monorhyme, the melody may be composed of phrases grouped according to all possible combinations.

This remark also applies to the songs of the trouvères. Among the songs written in French, one sees, at the same time, a naive, spontaneous inspiration and an elementary structure. This seems to bear witness to, if not a popular origin, at least to a popular dissemination. We cite, for example, one which is a veritable musical jewel. It is probable that the first verse of a song cited by Johannes de Grocheo in his *Theoria* is identical with this song. Applying the rules that we have devised for the interpretations of modes, here is a transcription of that song:

Quand le rossignol chante,-Qui nous charme par son chant, -Pour ma belle, douce amie-Je vois mon coeur rossignolant. -Jointes mains je la supplie, -Car jamais je n'aimai tant; -Je sais bien, que, si elle m'oublie, -C'en est fini di mon bonheur.

When the nightingale sings,/who charms us with his song,/for my fair, sweet love/my heart too sings like the nightingale./With hands joined I beg her mercy,/for never have I loved so much;/I know well, that, should she banish me,/it would be the end of all my joy.

This little masterpiece must have been a popular song of its day. The text is directly inspired by the concept of courtly love. This song has all the desirable qualities which are so lacking in our modern counterparts. It is a simple song, with two repeated musical phrases perfectly suited for singing. A discrete melancholy pervades the whole. Its composition in the key of G minor is consistent with the delicacy of the words.

Another French song, anonymous like the preceding one, moves us to compassion for the poet's desperate longing for the object of his desires:

Je suis heureux de pleurer en chantant,-Plus qu'en nulle manière,-Pour calmer ma douleur,-Qui ainsi me domine.-Cent soupirs je fais chaque jour,-C'est ma rente assurée.-L'unique joie que j'ai de l'amour-Me vient de mon allégeance.-Chacun dit que je suis fou,-Mais nul ne le sait mieux que moi.

I am happy to weep while singing,/it is the only way/to calm this sadness/which engulfs me./I sigh one hundred sighs a day,/this is my allowance./The only joy I get from love/comes from my faithfulness./Everyone says that I am foolish,/but no man knows this better than I.

The same melancholy, felt so deeply and expressed so powerfully in the poignant movement of the second mode, the same sighs so touching in their resignation, are found in various lovers' plaints, in Provençal and well as French.

But we cannot linger over the *canso*, whatever our attachments. It is time to pass on to the political song and the poetic debate.

2. THE POLITICAL OR MORAL SONG (*SIRVENTES*)

HE *Doctrina de Compondre Dictatz*, which we have referred to previously, speaks in the following way about this genre: "To make a *sirventes*, it is necessary to speak of warfare, speak well or badly of someone, or relate current facts. The author shall borrow the verse form, the rhymes and stanzas from a good song whose melody, likewise, he shall make use of. He shall preserve the number of syllables from the original, but will be allowed to modify the order of the rhymes".

This definition indicates that the *sirventes* is the antithesis of the *canso*. The love song expresses the most intimate sentiments of the poet, which no one else is able to share, and few are capable of understanding. The melodic expression of this feeling is therefore always original. In the sirventes, on the contrary, the troubadour depicts feelings which he shares among all his political partisans. The admiration or indignation which a political event arouses has little to do with the personal. All who are shocked by the excesses of a party in power express the same anger, just as all who approve of a prince experience similar sympathies. Certainly, the degree of emotional reaction varies according to the temperament of the individual, but the fundamental emotion rarely bears a personal stamp. It is for this reason that it is unnecessary to form original poetic or musical expressions for a purely social sentiment. When collective feelings are being expressed, it is possible to spare the effort that would go into delineating one's most intimate feelings. Assuredly, a love of art, or perhaps professional ambition, may have compelled a troubadour to compose an original *sirventes*, but he was never obliged to do such. And for this reason, the most celebrated masters of the political song did not hesitate to borrow verses. The most ardent and opinionated among them, Bertran de Born (1159–1196), comments himself that he composed one of his most caustic *sirventes*, the one concerning 'the young king" Henry III of England, 'king of roques'', upon a melody derived from a debate between Guiraut de Borneilh and Alamande: *Conselh vuolh dar el so de n'Alamanda* (I would like to make known to you Lady Alamande's melody). Likewise, Uc de Saint-Cirec (1200–1256) begins a *sirventes: Un sirventes vuolh far en aquest so d'en Gui* (I would like to compose a *sirventes* on this melody of Lord Guy). According to the *Doctrina*, it is precisely this characteristic of the *sirventes*, its lack of originality, from which the name of the genre is derived. The *sirventes* is so called because one is served a song, from which one may then help themselves to the use of the melody and words. *Sirven* in Provençal means the "servant". Therefore, *sirventes* means that which has the characteristics of a servant. This explains why so few manuscripts preserve the melodies of *sirventes*. The performer was expected to know the melody.

To give an idea of the nature of the *sirventes*, we shall cite the first verse of a satirical song by Peire Cardenal (first half of the thirteenth century). In this song the misanthropic poet hates women because he has never been loved, loaths society because it is corrupt and false, begrudges the crusaders because they are debauched and murder innocent people, condemns the clergy for its greed, gluttony and addiction to luxury, and attacks even the Creator as a protest against the pains of hell and purgatory.

The melody is as unique as the text. Peire enjoys embellishing the notes and rhymes. When he addresses his recrimination to God, instead of assuming the air of a penitent, he elevates the melody and exclaims with all his force, *Senhar, merce, no sia* (Lord, please, let it not be so). Here he has a change of mind; he assumes an air of entreaty and submission to ask pardon for his sins. This only serves to emphasize the oddness of the first exclamation. On the whole, the song presents an irresistible comic effect.

A new *sirventes* intends to begin,/which I shall proclaim on judgement day/to him who shall deliver me from naught,/should he denounce me for my faults./And if to the devil he commit my soul/I shall cry, Lord, have pity on me,/I suffered so harshly in the world,/please preserve me from torment now.

This fine satire was not the only one to offer resistance to the structure of society and the representatives of spiritual authority. A number of troubadours had the courage to utter denunciations against false priests. Even among the most ancient polyphonic compositions, there is to be found a Latin motet of the twelfth century directed against "pseudopontifical hypocrites", which incorporates daring epithets and rude vocabulary aimed against servants of the church.

The *sirventes* form an independent literary genre, and in manuscript they are usually collected together in a separate fascicle.

The *Song of the Crusade*, in which the poet invites Christians to join in a holy war, belongs to the category of *sirventes*. From a musical point of view, these songs are inferior to many others. The fervor of the words, alone, seems to dominate the melodic structure. This inferiority may derive from the fact that these songs were usually addressed to the masses of the people, who for the most part were totally lacking in culture. Since the songs of the crusade have already been admirably edited by Joseph Bédier, we refer the reader to this edition, in which the melodies are transcribed, according to my own system of modal interpretation, by P. Aubry.

The *enueg* (ennui) approaches the nature of the *sirventes*, since the poet, expressing his annoyance, implicitly criticizes the conditions of life and the conventions of society. One example of this genre, of which we present only the first verse, has an improvisational character, delivered by a clown who has been fortified by the fruit of the vine.

colp noi a a- gut, Ca-pe- la e mor-gue bar-
un seul coup re- çu, Cha-pe- lain et moi- ne bar-

but, E lau-zen- gier bec es-mo- lut.
bu, Et mé- di- sant au bec ai- gu.

I am annoyed, if I dare say so,/by the vile language of gentlemen/and by his fellow-being who wishes to destroy./It annoys me, as does a horse who draws the reigns,/and I am annoyed by my poor health,/By the adolescent who carries a shield/though without having received a single blow/and by the chaplain and bearded monk,/by the sharp nosed slanderer.

This is followed by further banalities, interspersed with additional "ennuis", which, even in the original text, we would hardly dare to print.

The author of this *enueg* was a religious man, the famous monk of Montaudon (c. 1200). He borrowed the melody for his jest from a long song by Bertran de Born, that sower of discord. Dante, in the eleventh canto* of the *Inferno*, depicts Bertran de Born carrying his severed head in his right hand, as a punishment for his politics, which constituted separating the sons from their father, the King of England. Bertran composed two funeral songs, *planhs*, on the death of the young king, Henry (1183).**

The *planh* is a song composed on the occasion of the death of a prince or some other political figure. Characteristically, it is more personal than either the *sirventes* or the *enueg*, since the troubadour is given the opportunity of expressing a grief common to all admirers, countrymen, and servants of the deceased. The music of only two of these *planhs* has been preserved. One is the *planh* of Gaucelm Faidit (1180–1216) on the death of Richard the Lion Hearted (1169–1199), and the other, by the last of the troubadours, Guiraut Riquier (1254–1292), composed in honor of Amauric IV of Narbonne (died 1270). Here is the first verse of the *planh* of Gaucelm Faidit; it should give the reader an idea of the nature of the genre, whose depth of emotion is reflected in the tragic accents of the melody.

*Translator's note—M. Beck is mistaken: Bertran de Born appears in canto twenty-eight of Dante's *Inferno*.
**Translator's note—That is, Prince Henry, who never came to the throne.

Texte orig. *Fortz chauza es que tot lo ma- ior*
Version adap· Quel deuil im- mense et quel cru- el mal-

dan *El ma- ior dol, las! qu'ieu anc*
heur Pour tous les siens, quel cha- grin

mais a- gues, E so don dei tos- temps pla-
sans pa- reil! Et moi, au lieu de pleu- rer

nher plo- ran, M'a- ven a dir en chantan
de dou- leur, Je dois chan- ter et di- re

e re- trai- re. Car selh qu'e- ra de
ma souf- fran- ce. Car lui, le prince et

va- lor caps e pai- re, Lo rics va-
le chef de vail- lan- ce, Le bon, le

lens Ri- chartz, reis dels Eng- les Es
grand Ri- chard, roi des An- glais, Est

mortz. Ai Dieus! quals perd' e
mort Oh Dieu! Re- grets à

quals dans es! Quant estrangz motz, quan salvatge
tout ja- mais! Mort! L'affreux mot, si terrible

a au- zir! Ben a dur cor totz
à ou- ïr! Bien dur ce- lui qui

hom qu'o pot suf- frir.
l'en- tend sans fré- mir.

What deep mourning and what cruel misfortune/for his heirs, what grief unequalled,/and for me, in lieu of sad weeping,/must sing and speak of my misery./For he, the prince and chief of gallantry,/the good, the great Richard, King of England, is dead./Oh God! I shall regret this forever./Dead! the horrible word, so terrible to hear./It is a hard man who can hear it without shuddering.

Among the works of Gaucelm Faidit, there also exist several poetical debates, *tensos*, a lyric genre with a discussion of which we shall conclude this chapter.

In the *tenso*, two characters discuss a question of gallantry, politics or morality. During the course of their development, these dialogue songs, which derive from the earliest troubadours, present a variety of types.

In its earliest form, the *tenso* was nothing but a *disputatio*, a discussion of any one of many questions. Among the *sirventes*, there are examples in which a poet composes a reply to the song of an adversary, preserving the verse and melodic form of his adversary. The same principle is found in the *tenso*, with one difference, that the discussion is divided into alternating verses within the same song. It is not necessary that the *tenso* should actually have two authors. In this way the monk of Montaudon, whose *enueg* we have previously cited, was able to contrive a discussion with God on the use of cosmetics among women.

In the *joc partit* (play in parts), the first verse announces the problem proposed by the poet. The following verses develop alternatives by two or three speakers, in the form of affirmative and negative explications. The subject matter, often humorous, is taken from various situations of life. The sophistry of love, with all its frivolity, represents the greater part. The troubadour who proposes the interchange also determines the melody. As in the *canso* and the *sirventes*, each of the verses in the *tenso* and *joc partit* is sung to the melody that is formulated in the first verse. The form of these debates necessitates the participation of at least two singers. In reality, it is possible that, once these songs were composed, they may have been performed by a single singer assuming all the roles—a less effective arrangement.

ERE we present a verse from a *joc partit* which was preserved by two different songwriters, one from Rome and the other from Sienna, utilizing two different melodies. This fact, not peculiar to this example, seems to indicate that each of the participants was free to make use of his own melody, unless of course, one was added at a later time. A notator may, in fact, have filled a lacunae in a manscript by adapting some other melody to the text. A third possibility is that the initiator of the metric and melodic structure may have suggested variations on the form.

The following verse is from the *joc partit* between Jehan Bretal (died 1272) and Grieviler, and is to be found in the Roman manuscript.

Grie- vi- ler, par maintes fi- es   Ai de-
A vous de main- tes par-ties, Or res-

man-dé et par- ti   Li- quels ai me
pon-dés a ches- li :

mieus a droit,   Ou cil qui si cler i voit

Qu'il set de-çoi- vre s'a- mi- e,   Ou cil

qui en li se fi- e   Tant qu'il se laist deche-

voir   Et ne le set perche- voir.

Grieviler, par maintes fois-Je vous ai demandé et proposé-Maintes parties; or répondez à celle-ci:-Lequel aime le mieux, au fond,-Celui qui est assez clairvoyant-Pour savoir tromper son amie,-Ou celui qui à elle se fie-Au point de se laisser tromper-Sans e'en apercevoir.

Grieviler, so many times/I have inquired of you and proposed/many debates, respond to them now./Who do you love the most, in all honesty,/he who is discerning enough/to be able to deceive his lover/or the one whom she trusts/to the point that she deceives herself/without knowing it.

The melodies of the *joc partit* are, in general, less ornate than those of the *canso*. The songs of courtly love are the vehicles of emotions, those of the *joc partit* of ideas, from which the simple but energetic tunes derive.

B. Narrative or Dramatic Songs

HE principal lyric forms which constitute the narrative or dramatic genre would appear to be of popular origin, and yet an examination of the music tends to contradict this speculation—a purely literary one. The music of the *alba* (dawn song) and of the historical songs is highly developed and seems to derive from the *Alleluia*. Many romances and pastorals follow, note for note, the tunes of sacred pieces. The music of the *alba* and historical song is, perhaps, the most accomplished of all troubadour music. This will become apparent after a study of the characteristics of the four varieties of this type of song.

1. The Dawn Song (*Alba*)

In the *alba*, with its repetition of the word "alba" (dawn) in the last line of each verse, the troubadour portrays the feelings that the approach of day arouses in lovers who are obliged to separate after a night of happiness.

During the long and dark night,/which is never too long for me,/I am, despite the cold weather,/a restless watchman over lovers' discretion./Until the first light I stand guard, to protect my friend,/then I urge with my cry:/Beware here comes the dawn.

No other composition of the middle ages exhibits such technical brilliance as do these songs. They show the profound influence of sacred music. The poetic texts, as well, display a certain religious imprint.

The famous *alba* of Guiraut de Bornelh (1175–1220), *Reis glorios, verais lums e clartatz*, begins with a majestic invocation to God. An example by Guilhelm d'Autpol (end of the thirteenth century), *Esperansa de totz ferms esperans*, whose music has not survived, is a prayer to the virgin, a prayer whose language strangely echoes the customary phraseology of the Latin *sequentiae*. The poetic text of the *alba* reproduced above, attributed to Foquet de Marseille (died 1237), or to his contemporary, Cadenet, does not have this religious association. The music, however, is identical, in certain passages, with the notes and general design of the majestic *alba*, *Reis glorios* by Guiraut.

2. Historical Songs, or *Chansons de Toile*

HE "history" which is sung in these poems, of which only five retain their melody, are anecdotes of a sentimental nature. They almost invariably concern a young girl, referred to as *belle* (beautiful), who is in a state of sorrow either because of her parents, the object of her affections, or because of the pitiless death which has deprived her of her lover. The majority of these songs depict *La Belle* engaged in some type of woman's work, sewing, weaving or spinning (hence the name *chanson de toile*, or "cloth song"). It is highly unlikely that they were composed to be sung by women while attending to their duties. The romance of *Guillaume de Dole* (thirteenth century) has preserved, among several other lyric pieces, a number of *chansons de toile*. One of which, entitled *La Belle Aiglentine* (Bartsch, Rom. u. Past. I number 2), was sung by a young man riding his horse along *la grant chaucie* (the open road); another is presented as being declaimed by the nephew of the Bishop of Liege (Bartsch, I, 13).

The delightful impression one receives from these songs is not contradicted by an analysis of their subject matter. The *belles* are of a gentle disposition, often of humble origin, and display a tenderness calculated to captivate any knight. *La Belle Isabeau* declares to her mother that despite the reproaches of her husband and of all her relatives she will not renounce her love for Count Mathieu, etc. This genre is not subject to as strict a formula as is the long song, but nevertheless, the knights behave themselves as courteously as do the authors of any of the *cansos*.

The difference in attitude may be the result of a difference in the objective of the song, i.e., the *chanson de toile* was meant to entertain a man when he was far from his lady, while the *canso* was to be addressed directly to a lady. A knight on a long journey would dispel his boredom by imagining a "belle". She would be less haughty than the noble lady whom he desperately longs to move to pity by means of the pathetic verses of his *canso*.

The song, *Belle Oriolant*, confirms these views. The trouvère terminates his "history" with this verse:

Je ne sais que plus vous en dire;-Qu'il en soit ainsi pour tous les amants.-Et moi qui fis cette chanson,-Pensif au bord de la mer,-Je recommande à Dieu la belle Aëlis.
    Refrain: Dieu! Que le bonheur vient lentement à celui qui le désire.

I do not think that I can say it again,/that it should be thus for all lovers./And for me who has made this song,/pensively by the sea alone,/I commend to God *la belle Aëlis*.
    Refrain: God! May happiness come slowly to him who desires it.

Be that as it may, these *chansons de toile* were not composed for, and certainly not by, spinning-girls, but rather by consummate poet-musicians. Here for example is the song *Belle Doette*, whose construction betrays such an expert's hand.

Belle Doette, à la fenêtre assise,-Lit dans un livre, mais son coeur n'y est pas.-De son ami Doon il lui souvient,-Qui en d'autres pays est allé querroyer.
Refrain: Et maintenant elle en a du chagrin.

Belle Doette, at her window seat,/is reading a book, but her heart's not in it./The book calls to mind her lover Doon,/who has gone far away to fight a war.
Refrain: And now she is so sad.

We can dispense with comments upon the literary character of this piece; it is a typical formula. The music, however, is of a rare delicacy. The skill of a scientist was required so successfully to put these verses to music, especially the grievous refrain, *et or en ai dol*. It seems unlikely that the complex vocalizations on the words *livre* and *terres* could have been executed within the confines of the women's chambers, such rhythms demand well trained artists. Such refined music as this excludes the possibility of a popular origin, or a popularization, of these songs. The only models which approximated this level of development were the modulations in the gregorian chant.

3. The Romance

HE romance does not perceptibly differ from the *chanson de toile*. Its inspiration and attitude towards love derive from a similar source. The love, however, is generally more frivolous than that of the *chanson de toile*, which implies a different musical emphasis. The melodies of the romance are lighter and more gracious. Furthermore, the author of the romance personally narrates his story, as if he had been present and witnessed the proceedings. It is for this reason that descriptions, especially those of the *belle*, play such a central role, as for example in this charming scene:

Gracieux, animé.

Vo- lez vos que je vos chant Un son d'amors a- ve- nant. Vi- lain nel fist mi- e, Ainz le fist un che- va- lier, Soz l'on- bre d'un o- li- vier, Entre les braz s'a- mi- e.

Voulez-vous que je vous chante-Un jolie chant d'amour?-Ce n'est pas un vilain qui l'a faite,-Mais la fit un chevalier,-Sous l'ombre d'un olivier,-Entre les bras de son amie.

Shall I sing you/a pretty song of love?/No common villein gave it life;/it was composed by a knight/underneath an olive tree,/wrapped in the arms of his true love.

This piece, so delicate and subtle, betrays the hand of a professional, down to the most superficial details. The mention of the olive tree, unknown in the *langue d'oil* country, but quite familiar to French imitators of the troubadours, supplies an exotic stamp. Musically, the melody is of the gregorian type. The beginning is characteristic of numerous religious songs (Antiennes, for example). It is not surprising that the author would choose his song from the repertory of the church, in order to ensure it as widespread a circulation as possible.

The following May Song is less etherial, poetically, than the romance, *Volez vos que je vos chant*. The melody, whose simplicity and naivity do not conceal the effort that went into its composition, is exquisite and surpasses that of the previous example. It is attributed to Moniot d'Arras, one of the more gifted trouvères of the thirteenth century.

Ce fut en Mai, -Au doux temps gai-Que la saison est belle./Tôt me levai-Jouer m'allai-Près d'une fontenelle.-En un verger-Clos d'églantier-Ouis un vielle-La, vis danser-Un chevalier-Et une damoiselle.*

It happened in May,/in the dear sweet time/when the season is lovely./I had risen myself/to make my getaway./Near the little fountain,/in an orchard/closed in with wild roses,/I heard an old woman/there, saw together dancing/a bold knight/and a beautiful lady.

*Translator's note—This song is the only instance were M. Beck has not provided a French translation. This French version was taken from Jean Maillard's anthology of trouvère songs.

4. The Pastoral and Dance Music

HE subject matter of the pastoral is openly libertine. The characters involved in this little drama are a shepherd girl and a knight—the poet himself, or some other. In most cases the shepherd girl expresses a degree of intelligence uncommon among keepers of geese and cattle. She is generally quite skillful at repelling her aristocratic seducer and ridiculing his thwarted efforts, often amongst other country folk. In those pastorals which have a more fulfilled ending, the libertinism is redeemed by a grace of form. Though these songs are seldom edifying, they are usually inoffensive. The music, light but deft, adds in its way a pleasantness to these unpretentious little compositions, considered among the most gracefull of medieval lyrics.

Près du bosquet de Loncpré-J'errais avant hier.-Là je vis se trémousser,-Le long d'un sentier,-Une jolie tousette,-Sage, plaisante et jeunette.-Dieu! tant fus ravi,-Quand seule la vis.-Et la fille tout ainsi-Se mit à chanter:-Robin, que je dois aimer,-Tu risques de tarder trop.

Near the arbor of Loncpré,/I was wandering the day before yesterday./There I saw, moving tremulously/along a pathway,/a pretty maiden,/intelligent, pleasant and young./God, I was enraptured,/to see her all alone./And as young girls will,/she began to sing to herself:/Robin, I should be loved,/it is a risk to wait too long.

The melody is characteristic of dance music. Notice how skillfully the composer introduces and develops the theme of the refrain within this verse. The opening phrase shares points in common with an anonymous instrumental piece inscribed incompletely in an early fourteenth century songbook. It is the opening of an *estampie*. There it is in its original notation:

In modern notation, this phrase would be transcribed as follows:

The *estampie* was composed of a certain number of minor themes alternating with a phrase which constitutes the refrain. In an article from the *Revue des Deux Mondes* (1906), Joseph Bédier, in an examination of dance songs, came to the conclusion that some of the songs that we have been studying in this chapter were meant to be mimed and performed as brief comedies. The justification for such a conclusion can be traced to several sources. A thirteenth century theoretician, Johannes de Grocheo, whom we have previously mentioned, informs us that the melodies of dance songs and dance tunes (*stantipes* and *ductia* in Latin, *estampida* and *dansa* in Provençal) inspired the listeners to make graceful movements which were called "dance"[1] and that these movements were regulated by the rhythmic accents of the compositions.

1. Exitant aninum hominis ad ornate movendum secundum artem quam ballare vocant.

The *Leys d'Amors* and the *Doctrina* are likewise clear on this subject. One finds a good number of pastorals and motets which are referred to as *estampida*. Furthermore, in manuscripts of the eleventh through the fourteenth centuries, one finds numerous representations of singers and dancers in positions unmistakably mimetic. If we formulate, from a musical point of view, strict relationships between certain pastorals and authentic dance tunes, it is necessary to conclude that these compositions were at the same time dance tunes and dramatic presentations. This dramatic element, in fact, is extremely important to the medieval lyric. In the *joc partit*, it is apparent that the retorts constitute veritable scenes with dialogue. May songs, pastorals, rondeaux and many other dance songs are, in actuality, pantomimes, melodramas and primitive forms of ballet.

C. Harmonized Songs — Motets

ITH the motet, we leave monodic composition aside and address ourselves to a study of the principles of harmony in the middle ages. The motet, according to Johannes de Grocheo, is a song for several voices with varied words for each voice, producing a continuous harmonic accord. Expanding upon his definition, Grocheo informs us that one of the voices, or parts—there may be two, three or even four—is designated tenor and sings no words. The principle voice bears the name of motet (*motettus, motellus*). The tenor part is a melodic phrase derived from the beautiful and seminal *alleluia*. Just as several words in the margin of an alleluia are enough to indicate the tune, so it is with the tenor: one never finds more than a general indication of the pitch.

The composer of the tenor line simultaneously preserves the melodic format of the *alleluia*, or whatever other musical model he made use of, and alters the rhythm to suit his own composition. If, for example, he were to chose the first mode as a response to the rhythm of the motet, he might fragment the original melodic phrase into a suite of little rhythmic themes

♩ ♩ ♪ ♩ ♩ ♩ ♪ . If he were using the second mode, the same sounds might follow in an inverse rhythmic pattern ♩ ♩ ♪ ♪ ♩ ♩ ♪ ♪ . If he incorporated the third mode, he might group the notes in a series of four, encompassing two measures ♩ ♪ ♩ ♩ ♪ ♪ ♩ ♪ ♩ ♩ ♪ ♪ . In other modes (for many more modes are made use of in the tenors of motets than are in songs), a completely different fashion of groupings is employed. In the motet, the different verses are not necessarily compelled to follow the rhythm of the tenor. Because of the absolute tertiary system of medieval rhythm, the cadence, for example of ♩ ♩ ♩ ♪ ♪ (the fifth mode), used in the tenor line would always agree with the other parts, whatever their modal structure.

From a harmonic point of view, the motet is the precursor of the counterpoint of the fugue. On the accented beat a perfect harmony (fifth, fourth or octave) is obligatory, dissonance being permitted only on the unaccented beat. The constant employment of perfect chords does not date back earlier than the fifteenth century.

As an example let us take two phrases from polyphonic compositions of the thirteenth century. The first is a *rondeau* theme, a dance tune, formed from several verses sung in an order determined by two interconnected musical phrases. The second

example is the opening of a Latin motet in honor of Saint Catherine, the melody of which, incidently, has been adapted to a number of popular songs.

These dissonances are hardly charming to the ear of the modern listener, accustomed as he is to the use of thirds and softer harmonies. However, the thirteenth century listener, unaccustomed to the use of the third and the sixth, must have accommodated himself to these erudite series of melodies.

From a rhythmic and melodic point of view, this polyphonic music possesses some rich and curious variations. Many poems were adapted to a melody in imitation of the *sequentiae* of the *alleluia*. The poet-musician would distribute the syllables of his new song, fragmenting groups of notes and supplying one syllable of text for each note, in the same manner as the monks did in their early *sequentiae*.

The first motets date from the end of the twelfth century. In the following century, this genre, derived from the descant in the church, developed prodigiously due to a contemporary demand for polyphonic music. This taste for the motet shouldn't be surprising: when sung in the vernacular language, the motet unites the qualities of troubadour song with those of the choir. Since the art of harmony is more rich in possibilities than is the art of monody, many excellant musicians seem to have been attracted to the genre. Among the authors of motets are to be found the likes of Moniot and Adam de la Halle, two master trouvère-composers of the thirteenth century.

While polyphonic music was soaring, troubadour poetry was on the decline. The theory of courtly love was turning into an idealized form of mysticism and was taking on a markedly religious character. In Italy, the theory was translated into the doctrine of the "sweet new style", the immortal Beatrice of Dante being a consummate example. In Provence, the movement came to an abrupt end with the poetry of Guiraut Riquier, the last of the troubadours. At this time, even in the libertine pastoral, one notices an increase of the purely religious spirit. Gautier de Coincy, for example, one of the most distinguished poets of the first half of the thirteenth century, addressed an older, secular pastoral to the Virgin by a careful reediting of several words.

In consequence of the popularity of *sequentiae* and motets in honor of the virgin, the secular song succumbed quite rapidly. During the two centuries of its brightest existence, the art of the troubadours had exhausted itself. Its decline was marked by a return to its sources.

E have in no way exhausted the subject. With more space available we could have discussed pious songs, the *lai*, a secular form of *sequentiae*, the *retrouange*, the *ballade*, the *rondeau* and other lyric genres in the category of light song. It is to be hoped that the examples we have given will provide at least a summary idea of troubadour music. More important, that they may awaken in the reader an appreciation of the older melodies. Contrary to changes in the poetic text, the music of medieval song has scarcely altered. Unless otherwise informed, one would doubt that these songs were drawn from the age of the crusades. The only thing which may be disconcerting to the modern ear is the absence of harmonic accompaniment. This lack has, we hope, been overcome in our forthcoming *Choix de Chansons de Troubadours*. We shall consider ourselves recompensed if our efforts effect a better understanding of the origins of these melodies from our oldest songbooks. It is our hope that they may stimulate those who, like us, seek their revival. There are more than two thousand troubadour songs, and among them true masterpieces. They wait patiently for whomever wishes to rescue them from the obscurity in which they have reposed for more than six centuries.

NEUF CHANSONS DE TROUBADOURS

Music transcribed by Walter Morse Rummel

English adaptation by Ezra Loomis Pound

French adaptation by M.D. Calvocoressi

Introduction by Michael Ingham

Introduction

ZRA Pound had established "make it new day by day" as a working principle long before he encountered it in Chinese ideograms; and though, to my knowledge, he never had it emblazoned on his bath tub, it was much more to him than some sort of Pre-Raphaelite bumper-sticker. It meant more, for example, than dressing up in Renaissance clothes and reconstructing harpsichords and whistles (however much he might have approved of this), and more than scholarship. It meant vitalizing for the time what is "permanent" in art.

Ernst Krenek in *Music Here and Now*:

> The texts [of Gregorian Chant] . . . determine the rhythms of the musical lines . . . Wherever the melodic line goes beyond the rhythm indicated by its text . . . such components are nothing more than variations and extensions of the shorter melodic features, directly created by the verbal accent. Their rhythmic outline is not decided by any force apart from the free articulation of the word.

> . . . periodic formulation (in which rhythmic and metric units predominate in balanced numbers . . .) is doubtless a principle which appears in sharp contrast to the free rambling manner of the Oriental structure [of Gregorian Chant].

RENEK goes on to show that much of the history of Western Music can be viewed as the opposition and intermingling of these two principles. It is only because "symmetrical scanning" (Krenek's term) was orthodoxy for three centuries in both poetry and music that the formulation of procedures for "free verse," or the deliberate destruction of regular meter in music (especially in setting prose or "free verse" texts) seemed at the beginning of this century so revolutionary. Pound had found his model in the Troubadours, and determined that symmetrical patterns are not requisites for sung verse. The Troubadours were the transmitters of some of the musical procedures of Gregorian Chant, but secular and uncodified, embodying a tradition both free and disciplined.

Though there is no sign of Pound's having noticed it, Claude Debussy expended in his opera *Pelléas el Mélisande* an energy at least equivalent in intensity and intelligence to Flaubert's labor for *le mot juste* in *Madame Bovary*. And

67

Debussy's product is as significant for music as Flaubert's is for literature. The barline had oppressed music for three centuries, reducing its bone to a series of deplorably anticipatable thumps. Poetry to be sung was either made to order for this inculcated pattern of four bar groups of 2, 3, 4, or 6 thuds per bar in a predetermined hierarchy of accentuation, or it was squeezed relentlessly to fit. Brahms merely poured a thick syrup over this problem of "the tyranny of the bar-line" with his constant hemiola, and Wagner accentuated it with his jingle-like libretti and eternal suspensions. Liszt appears to have been well on his way to its solution, and probably Debussy caught the drift of his efforts. But what is now common abandonment of that dreadful symmetry, especially as it relates to the word, can be said to have begun significantly with *Pelléas*.

A musical performer's technical mastery of the printed score is not the same as an understanding of it. It is his responsibility not only to understand it, but to manifest that understanding as unambiguously as possible in his execution. This involves the acquisition of a knowledge of the score which will enable him to perform it as though he had actually composed it. (All great performers make us feel they are inventing the music on the spot.) The "un-notatable" ideas must be made intelligible in sound, and this is accomplished through the articulation of agogic, dynamic, and tonic stresses—written and interpretive. The understanding of a piece of music is tantamount to the understanding of its accents. This is true for instrumental music, and doubly so for vocal music, because the text has its own articulatory demands, running often parallel with those of the music, but at times obliquely, and even directly counter to them. As in all counterpoint, this is a process of tensions and resolutions. It is the singer's burden to decipher the articulatory demands of both text and music, and to know at each moment of the music's progress what element must dominate, and to establish that ordering of degree among all stresses, so that each phrase emerges with the discernable shape the composer meant it to have. (The performer's work is like that of the translator. It is not difficult to think of Pound's translations as performances designed to make us forget alienations of time, culture, and language in our discovery of the new poem.) The difference for the singer in "interpreting" songs from say, the Elizabethans, versus those of the centuries of "symmetrical scanning"—Schubert, for example—is that in the former the textual and musical articulatory demands inter-react only with each other, and not, as in the latter, also with a constantly repeated pattern of accents predetermined by the meter.

Pound was astute in his rejection of sung texts of the baroque, classical and Romantic periods, which indeed were composed in "the sequence of the metronome, and not in the sequence of the musical phrase." Songs of Jacobean and Elizabethan composers revealed to Pound the principle that the integration of poetry and music enriches both, especially when this integration is accomplished in the mind of a single artist, as, for example, Thomas Campion. How much more then must this hold true for the Troubadours, for whom words and music were inseparable. It is no wonder that Pound dug in the Milan Library for the tunes to poems he knew were incomplete by themselves. Nor is it surprising that he made English versions which stand as poems and at the same time are singable. (Those of us who have labored for years to sing opera in English translation know what virtuosity this requires; and opera gives space in which to work, while song requires a hairsplitting exactitude.)

The re-issue of *Neuf Chansons de Troubadours* in this volume is significant as a testament to the skill of one of the greatest poetic craftsmen of this or any other age. The appearance of some of the texts as poems, without music, in Hugh Kenner's *Ezra Pound: Translations* gives no hint of the extent to which Pound preserved metrical and quantitative values. Nor did he throw out the meaning to "save the jingle". The most difficult technical task any poet could set for himself is met here with bravado. Speaking as a singer who has labored with many more or less inept translations, trying to get the meaning across through a tangle of misplaced accents, superfluous filler words, and clusters of awkward consonants, I can testify that with these versions one feels, while singing them, that the words invented the music.

Pound—hate as he might the mushy subject matter of *Pelléas*—is connected to Debussy by Walter Morse Rummel. Rummel earned his place in musical history by giving the premiere performance of Debussy's *Twelve Studies* to the enthusiastic approval of the composer. As Debussy was almost never satisfied with any performer's work, this is potent testimony to Rummel's skill and integrity as a pianist. His work as a composer, however, has proved ephemeral. These settings of *Neuf Chansons de Troubadours*, though carefully crafted, are not particularly memorable; and though they insist on exact execution of the rhythms (in ignorance of present musicological opinion that the rhythmical values of the Troubadours were very freely articulated), and though they rely almost exclusively on triple meter, the words and tunes do provide "permanent" values. If these songs were "made new" for Edwardian Paris and London in the form of salon music, why should we object? Pound was instigating. The place to instigate was the decaying, pleasant, often vital, Edwardian salon. It is difficult to measure the potency of these instigations. Though performers and audiences now, for the most part, remain rooted in the centuries of metrical symmetry, we can see about us, if we take the trouble to look, resurgences of metrical understanding worthy of the Troubadours and their integral freedom in casting words and music in one piece—to name only the most important, the songs and operas of composer/poet Ernst Krenek.

Ezra Pound was himself a vortex, and *Neuf Chansons de Troubadours* are merely one of a dense node of vectors radiating outward and stirring in us the will to act, to "make it new" for ourselves.

Walter Morse Rummel

(1912)

Hesternae Rosae

SERTA II.

Neuf Chansons de Troubadours des XIIième et XIIIième Siècles
pour une voix avec accompagnement
de Piano

Adaptation française par M. D. Calvocoressi
Adaptation anglaise par Ezra Pound

PREFACE

UNDER the collective title of *Hesternæ Rosæ* (Roses of Yesterday) the writer intends to gather whatever interesting and unknown material he may come across in his study of the music of the early and late past.

It is apparently necessary to mention here that this collection in no way contains scholastic or historical records. The writer's only aim has been, in a small way, to bring forward to the listener some of the beauties of old music: to set these melodic gems in what seems to him the most sympathetic and expressive pattern and surroundings.

No attempt has been made to limit the realisation of the following works; or to pay homage to any dry and stale dogmas scientifically imposed on a most delightfully living music by certain text-books to harmony and counterpoint.

To reflect some of the charm and atmosphere of these various works and melodies; to bring them before the public of to-day in as living and vital a form as possible—the form best adapted to our modern times—is the writer's only wish and intention.

The first volume (Nine French Songs of the 17th Century) is here followed by a collection of Nine Troubadour Songs of the 12th and 13th Centuries.

They are selected at random from the 259 now collected melodies, a treasure from which the writer hopes to draw frequently in the near future. Several of the songs here appear for the first time in a musically-practical setting and are selected from the Manuscripts of the "Bibliothèque Nationale" of Paris. The two Daniel melodies are here published for the first time to the writer's knowledge, and he is indebted to Mr. Ezra Pound, M.A., for communicating them from the Milan Library.

The musical notation of all of these melodies is *Neumatic* (by nods or signs), and bears no trace of rhythmic indications, save for occasional vertical lines which are supposed to have indicated pauses. The rhythmic re-constitution of such melodies is therefore, for lack of more positive records, a somewhat hypothetical task.

A translation of the metre of the words into the rhythm of music or the correct adherence of the tonal to dynamic accents, seems the most plausible and most admitted method of realising the rhythmic structure of this music, as by this process the notes very readily fall into the swing given to them by the metre of the words.

We find that the Troubadour was the miraculous combination of poet, musician, and in many cases performer. He, therefore, must have esteemed and loved his melodies as much as he did his verses, and he must have tried to find the most perfect harmony between the two arts.

This harmony was gradually lost in the centuries that followed, and at the end of the 16th Century, at the time when Instrumental Music became divorced from Vocal Music, the harmony between words and music was quite annihilated.

PRÉFACE

SOUS le titre collectif de "Hesternæ Rosæ" (Roses d'hier), l'auteur a l'intention de réunir peu à peu les mélodies et chansons oubliées ou inédites qui, venantà sa connaissance au cours de ses travaux sur la musique ancienne, lui sembleront dignes d'être remises au jour.

Il tient à dire ici que cette collection ne renfermera point de commentaires scholastiques ou historiques; que son seul but, en la publiant, est de faire revivre autant qu'il sera en son pouvoir, quelques unes des beautés de la musique ancienne, et qu'il ne fait que chercher à donner à ces joyaux musicaux la monture qui lui semble la plus apte à en faire ressortir le caractère et l'expression.

Il n'essaye de s'imposer aucune règle ni de rendre hommage à des dogmes infligés au nom de la science par certains manuels d'harmonie et de contrepoint à une musique, somme toute, délicieusement vivante.

Son unique intention est de conserver à ces différentes mélodies et chansons leur caractère particulier, d'évoquer le charme et l'ambiance de leur époque, et de les présenter au public sous une forme aussi libre que possible, forme adaptée à notre sentiment moderne.

Les "Neuf Chansons de Troubadours des 12ième et 13ième Siècles," qui font suite aux "Neuf Chansons du 17ième Siècle" (premier volume de cette publication) ont été prises presque au hasard dans les 259 mélodies de cette époque qu'on peut trouver actuellement dans les Bibliothèques: véritable trésor dans lequel l'auteur a l'intention de puiser fréquemment dans l'avenir.

Plusieurs de ces chansons, copiées d'après les manuscrits de la Bibliothèque Nationale de Paris paraissent pour la première fois dans ce recueil sous une forme musicalement pratique, et l'auteur croit pouvoir avancer que les deux chansons de *Daniel* n'ont jamais été publiées. Elles proviennent de la Bibliothèque de Milan, et l'auteur est redevable à Mr. Ezra Pound, M.A., de les lui avoir communiquées.

La notation musicale de toutes ces mélodies est neumatique (par signes) et ne porte pas trace d'indications rythmiques, à l'exception de quelques lignes verticales qu'on suppose devoir indiquer des pauses. La reconstitution rythmique de semblables mélodies est donc, faute de documents plus positifs, une tâche reposant sur des données plus ou moins hypothétiques.

Adapter le rythme de la musique à la métrique des mots, ou autrement dit, faire concorder l'accent tonique avec les accents dynamiques, semble la méthode la plus plausible à employer pour rétablir la structure rythmique de cette musique, les notes suivant ainsi très naturellement le rythme des mots.

Tout porte à penser que le troubadour devait réunir en lui, par une combinaison quasi miraculeuse, à la fois un poète, un musicien et, dans bien des cas, un exécutant. Il devait donc attacher autant de prix à sa mélodie qu' à sa poésie, et il a dû chercher à réunir les deux arts dans la plus parfaite harmonie

The unfolding of the music of the Troubadour must have therefore followed closely the rhythm of the text. The music (a chaos of written notes without definite outline or duration) shapes itself by this process into distinct groups having a distinct rhythm and beat.—

A characteristic of the mediæval music was the so-called *ligature*, or grouping of several notes on but one syllable of the text :—

son

These ligatures seem not to have been governed by any rhythmic law and in a way resembled our grace notes. They could be sung either slowly or fast, stretched out indefinitely or condensed into quick grace-notes. Following are but two of the many ways of realising such ligatures :—

Let us not forget that in old music, a great part was left to the imaginative quality of the interpreter, to improvisation ; that taste played a far greater rôle in the interpretation of that music than it did later on; that probably the distribution of these ligatures within the song form remained more or less a matter of the performer's taste.

The writer with the help of Mr. Ezra Pound, an ardent proclaimer of the artistic side of mediæval poetry, has given these melodies the rhythm and the ligature, the character which, from an artistic point of view, seems the most descriptive of the mediæval spirit.

Little light as the manuscripts of the Middle Ages throw on these melodies, they are still more obscure as to their setting with other instruments But space does not permit us to enter thoroughly into this long and problematic question.

It seems to the writer that there are some melodies, like almost all melodies of the Ancients, that do not permit of a regular substantial harmonisation. The only admissable method of harmonising these melodies would be by employing the Greek *Symphonia*, a harmony excluding all intervals save 4ths, 5ths and 8ves, and in tolerating only the other intervals should they appear as mere notes of passage.

possible. Cette harmonie s'est graduellement perdue pendant les siècles qui suivirent et se trouva complètement annihilée à la fin du 16ième Siècle, quand la musique vocale divorça définitivement d'avec la musique instrumentale.

La musique des troubadours devait donc être étroitement unie au texte. Si l'on adapte le rythme de la mélodie à celui du vers, cette musique, qui semble au premier abord un chaos de notes sans forme rythmique ni durées, prend forme d'elle-même et se divise en groupes distincts, ayant chacun leurs rythmes et leurs mesures distincts.

Une des caractéristiques de la musique médiévale est la *ligature*, ou groupe de plusieurs notes sur la même syllabe :

son

Ces ligatures semblent n'avoir été réglées par aucune loi rythmique. On pourrait les interpréter de diverses manières, soit étalées, soit précipitées comme des petites notes, selon les exemples donnés ci-après :—

N'oublions pas que, dans la musique ancienne, une grande part était laissée à l'imagination de l'interprète, à l'improvisation ; que le goût jouait un plus grand rôle dans l'interprétation de la musique qu'il ne le fît plus tard. Il est donc fort probable que la façon d'exécuter ces ligatures était laissée plus ou moins au goût du chanteur. L'auteur, avec l'aide de Mr. Ezra Pound, un ardent apôtre de l'art poétique médiéval, a donné à ces mélodies le rythme, et à ces ligatures le caractère qui, au point de vue purement artistique, lui ont paru exprimer le mieux l'esprit de l'époque.

Si les manuscrits du Moyen Age nous donnent peu de lumière sur les mélodies de cette période, ils sont encore plus obscurs en ce qui concerne leur accompagnement instrumental.

Les limites de cette préface ne nous permettent pas de traiter ici à fond de cette question. L'auteur pense que certaines de ces mélodies, comme presque toutes les mélodies de l'Antiquité, ne comportent pas d'harmonisation proprement dite. La seule méthode admissible pour harmoniser de semblables mélodies serait d'employer la *symphonie* des Grecs, n'admettant que la quarte, la quinte et l'octave, et ne tolérant les autres intervalles que s'ils se présentent sous la forme de notes de passage. Les harmoniser plus

To harmonise more substantially such melodies would be forcing disastrous surroundings on their delicate constitution.

Other melodies carry already within them the germ, which, under the guise of counterpoint, steadily unfolded, till during the 17th Century it arose victoriously, overgrew and choked counterpoint. This latter kind of melody has been harmonised. However, it may not be amiss to recall at this point a few interesting facts which are too often left unmentioned and which refer to the manner in which the writer has harmonised the latter kind of melody.

Tonality, which supplanted modality, brought with it the *deification* of one at the expense of six other and former great scales of the Ancients. This one scale, the so-called *Lydian* Scale, was itself transformed into the *Major* Scale and was destined to be the despotic ruler over all secular music. In this scale one tone (the tonic) was made to magnetise all the remaining six tones and to employ them for its own services. At a given period the seven old scales known to the Ancients under the aspect of the seven wondrous planetary gods were judged, perhaps found guilty of having hand in some pagan deviltry and were banished, only to return in an age which is more free from a certain dogmatism than the remarkable and yet in many ways destructive brilliance of the *Renaissance* and its influence.

This Major Scale, the rather materialised and personal god of our classical music, bringing with it many laws such as those concerning the seventh step or leading tone, the resolutions, cadences, all the outcome of the tempered system, gave rise to a most dogmatic science of harmony. It was firmly and despotically established in secular music soon after the Renaissance.

As to the freedom employed in the interludes of of the acccmpaniment, the writer wishes to remind the reader again that before music became dogmatic and over-scientific it was half an improvisational art. The last traces of this very old custom of creative interpretation of music disappeared with the 17th Century (the Figured Bass)

As to the rendering of these melodies, the writer wishes to point out that in employing measures in the re-constitution of the melodies he had in a few cases (mainly in the translations) to place unaccentuated syllables on the first beat, which, however, does not indicate necessarily that these syllables should receive a blow. Bars, a mere matter of mental convenience, when too materialised become destructive. In reciting these verses before singing them the interpreter will understand how to remedy this apparent deficiency in the prosody.

The writer desires in no way to impose on the reader his agogic and dynamic indications; music as this must be saturated with the interpreter's own personality, and does not stand a mere reading.

The writer wishes to extend his heartiest thanks to M. A. Jeanroy of the Faculty of Letters at the Paris University, for his kindness in facilitating matters for him.

W. M. R.
1912.

substantiellement serait les écraser sous un appareil trop lourd, incompatible avec leur délicate texture.

D'autres de ces mélodies portent déjà en elles le germe harmonique qui, sous forme de contrepoint, s'est développé graduellement jusqu'à éclore victorieusement au 17ième Siècle, époque où il détrône le contrepoint. L'auteur a donc harmonisé ces mélodies.

A ce propos il ne sera peut-être point inutile de rappeler ici quelques points intéressants, trop souvent passés sous silence et qui se rapportent à la manière dont l'auteur a harmonisé cette dernière catégorie de mélodies.

La tonalité, qui a supplanté la modalité, a entraîné la *déification* d'un seul mode, au détriment de six autres modes fondamentaux de l'Antiquité. Ce mode, le mode lydien, a été transformé en mode majeur et destiné à gouverner despotiquement toute la musique profane.

Dans ce mode, un son, la tonique, fut appelé à régner sur les six autres sons, et à faire de ceux-ci ses sujets. Les sept modes anciens, symboles dans l'Antiquité des sept dieux planétaires, furent peut-être, à une certaine époque, reconnus coupables d'avoir participé à quelque sorcellerie païenne, et, en conséquence, condamnés et bannis, pour ne réapparaître qu'à une époque plus dégagée d'un certain dogmatisme que celle de la *Renaissance*, dont l'influence éclatante fut souvent aussi destructive.

Ce mode majeur, le dieu matérialisé et personnel de notre musique classique, apportant avec lui de nombreuses lois nouvelles, comme celles concernant le septième degré ou note sensible, les résolutions, les cadences, résultant toutes du système à tempérament, donna naissance à une science harmonique des plus dogmatiques. Il fut fermement et despotiquement établi dans la musique profane peu après la Renaissance.

En ce qui concerne la liberté avec laquelle sont traités les interludes dans l'accompagnement, l'auteur rappelle encore une fois au lecteur que la musique fut autrefois, au moins en grande partie, un art d'improvisation. Les dernières traces de cette très ancienne interprétation créatrice ne disparaissent en Europe qu'avec le 17ième Siècle (basse chiffrée).

Quant à la manière de chanter ces chansons, l'auteur tient à faire remarquer qu'en employant des barres de mesures dans la reconstitution de ces mélodies, il a dû parfois, principalement dans les traductions, placer des syllabes non accentuées sur le premier temps, ce qui n'indique pas nécessairement que ces syllabes doivent être accentuées. La barre de mesure, qui n'est qu'une simple concession pratique, devient nuisible si on la prend dans un sens trop matériel. En récitant les vers avant de les chanter, l'interprète comprendra de quelle manière il doit remédier à ces apparentes fautes de prosodie.

L'auteur ne veut en aucune façon imposer rigoureusement ses indications agogiques et dynamiques. Cette musique doit être imprégnée de la personalité de son interprète et ne supporte pas d'être simplement traduite telle qu'elle est écrite.

L'auteur prie M. A. Jeanroy, Professeur à la Faculté des lettres de l'Université de Paris, de trouver ici l'expression de sa reconnaissance pour l'obligeance qu'il lui a témoignée.   W. M. R.
1912.

I.
CHANSSON DOIL MOT.

Arnaut Daniel.

[fin du XIIième siècle.]

*) Note pour toutes les chansons: Les petites notes doivent tomber partout *sur* le temps.

II.
LO FERM VOLER.

Arnaut Daniel.
[fin du XII<u>ième</u> siècle.]

III.

QUANT L'HERBA FRESQ EL FUELL APAR.

Bernart de Ventadour.

[milieu du XIIième siècle.]

Très simple.

CHANT.

PIANO.

toujours au second plan, mais bien soutenu.

Quant   l'her _ ba   fresq   el   fuell   a _ par   El
Quand   naît   la   jeu _ ne   feuille   au_ bois,   Et
When   grass   starts   green   and   flow _ ers__ rise   A-

fuels   es _ pan _ dis   pel   ver _ jan   El   ros _ sin _ hol__ au
quand   ver _ dis _ sent   les   val _ lons   Du   ros _ si _ gnol__ la
leaf   in   gar _ den   and   in__ close   And   phi _ lo _ mel__ in

tet   el   clar   Aus _ sa   sa   votz__ e   mou   son__ chan.
dou _ ce   voix   Mo _ dule   au   loin__ de   gaies   chan _ sons.__
dul _ cet   cries   And   lift _ ed   notes__ his   heart   be _ stows.__

espress.

*) Voir la page 1.

IV.
LAS GRANS BEAUTATZ.

Folquet de Romans (Rotmans)

[commencement du XIIIième siècle]

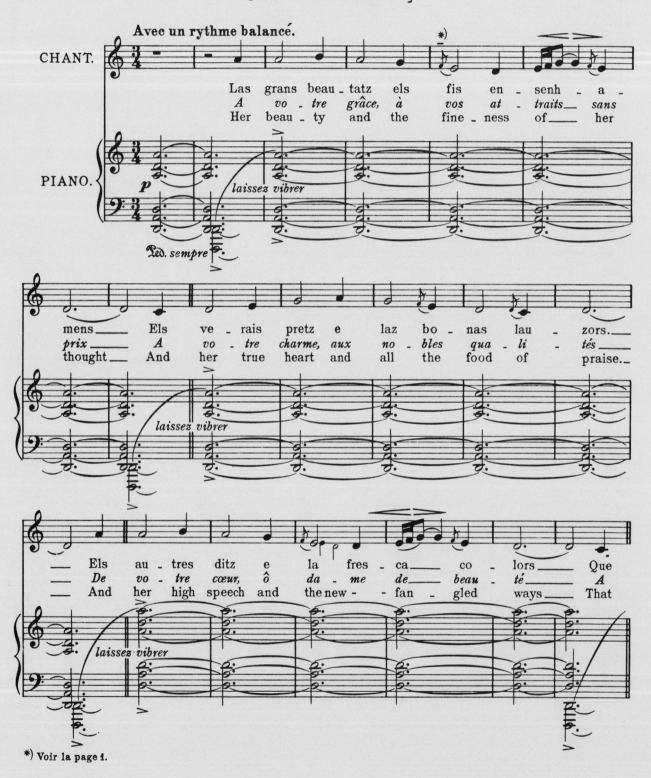

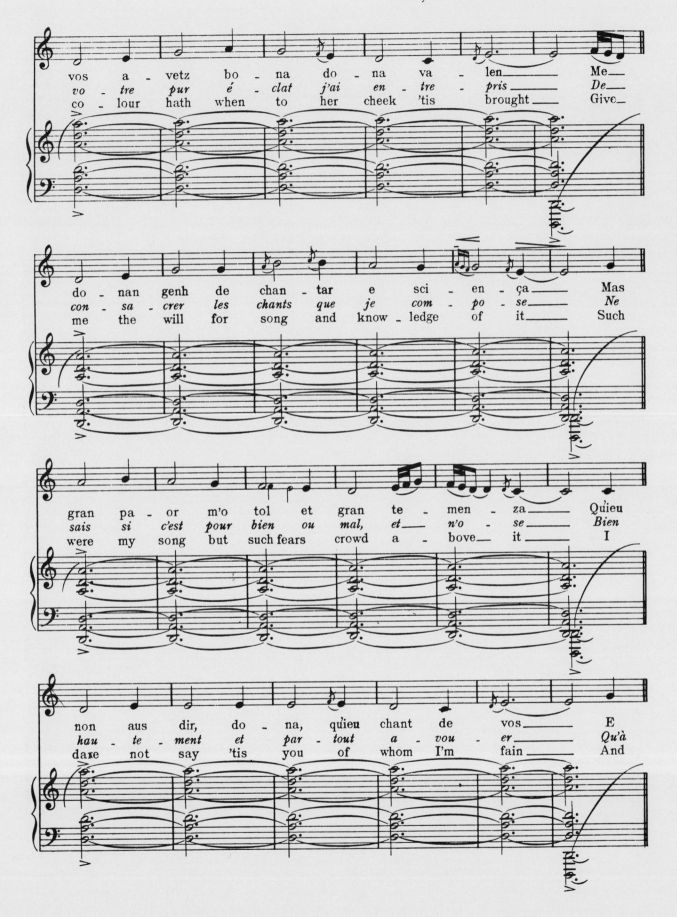

V.
TANT M'ABELIS.

B. de Palazol.
[milieu du XIIᵉᵐᵉ siècle.]

Tant m'a _ be _ lis joys et a _ mors et chans_____ Et a _ le _ grier, de _ port et cor _ te _ zi _ a_____ Quel mon non a _ ri _ cor ni
Si doux me sont bon _ heur, a _ mour et chant_____ Jo _ yeux é _ bats et cour _ toise al _ lé _ gres _ se_____ Qu'il n'est puis_sance au mon _ de
So plea _ seth me joy and good love and song_____ And mer _ ri _ ment, fine ways and gen_tle breed _ ing._____ Nor sil _ ver nor rich rent has

*) Note. Retenir légèrement les deux dernieres mesures de chaque vers de cette chanson.

VI.

MERE AU SAUVEOUR.

Williaume li Viniers.
[milieu du XIIIième siècle.]

Dans le style d'un Recit, très librement.

*) Voir page 1.

VII.

LI GRANZ DESIRS.

Li Cuens d'Angou.

[milieu du XIIIième siècle.]

Simple, pas trop lent.

Li granz de _ sirs et la dou _ ce pen _ sé _ _ e, Que
Le grand dé _ sir et la dou _ ce pen _ sé _ _ e Que
The great de _ sire sheds fragrance o'er my think _ _ ing. My

j'ai pour_ vos, da _ me qui_ va _ lez tant_____ Dont la pai _
j'ai pour_ vous, da _ me qui_ va _ les tant_____ Dont la pei _
thought for_ you, Ma _ dame, who'rt worth so much_____ Hath in it

ne ne puet es _ tre cé _ lé _ _ e Ou_ m'a _ vez _ mis et
ne ne peut ê _ tre cé _ lé _ _ e Où_ m'a _ ves mis et
pain 'gainst which there is no blink _ _ ing, You have me made and

*)Voir la page 1.

VIII.

MAINTA IEN ME MAL RAZONA.

Pierol.

[fin du XIIième siècle.]

IX.
A L'ENTRADE.

Chanson à danser
de la fin du XIIième siècle.

*) Voir page 1.

en _ tre nos   en _ tre   nos. _____
tout gaî _ ment   en _ tre   nous! _____
our own way,   our own   way. _____

Plus vite.

Mas   pir nei _ ent   lo vol far
Mais   la belle   aux   yeux mu _ tins
But   our sweet _ est   la _ dy here,

Au mouvement.

glissando

eya! _____   K'el _ e n'a soing   de viell _ art   eya! _____
eya! _____   *Pour   le vieux n'a   que dé _ dain*   *eya!* _____
eya! _____   Hath   of old men   lit _ tle care,   eya! _____

Mais   d'un le _ gier   ba _ che _ lar   eya! _____   Ki   ben sa _ che
Le   beau jou _ ven _ ceau qui vient,   *eya!* _____   *Sau _ ra di _ ver,*
And   for light-foot bäch _ e _ lors,   eya! _____   Keep _ eth she that

LIST OF SONGS

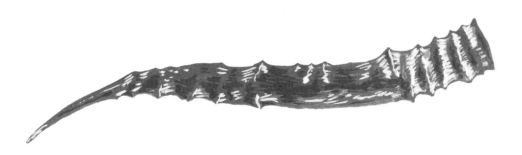

GUILHEM IX: TEXTS AND TRANSLATION

Translated by John D. Niles

Introduction, Textual Notes and Commentary
by John D. Niles

Plate II

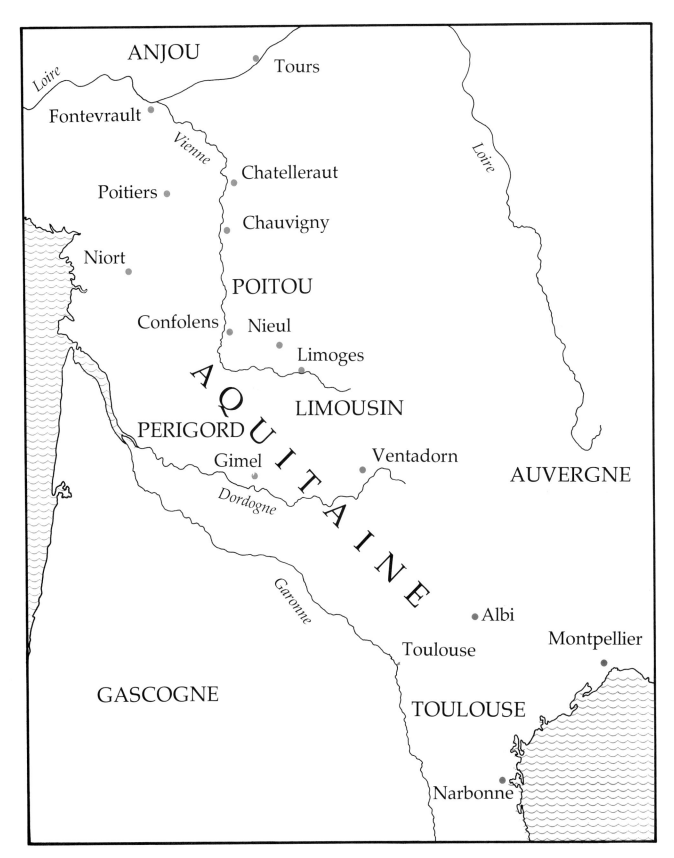

THE FRANCE OF GUILHEM IX

Introduction

good deal of what is thought of as modern literature could be said to begin with Guilhem de Peitieus (1071–1127), author of the ten earliest extant troubadour songs. As the seventh Count of Poitiers and the ninth Duke of Aquitaine, Guilhem held lands more extensive than those of any other ruler of his day in France, the King of France not excepted. As the first of the known troubadours, he stands at the head of a tradition of human sensibility which was to dominate much of the intellectual and emotional life of the Occident for some eight hundred years after his death. It was he, as far as we know, who first popularized a concept of woman as the object of idealized love. At the same time, he was masterful in exploring love as the theme of bawdy comedy. Twice married, twice excommunicated, twice a crusader, he seems to have lived a full and sometimes irreverent life, and his descendants (including his granddaughter Eleanor of Aquitaine and her children King Richard the Lion-Hearted, King John, and Marie de Champagne) followed his example in sponsoring a kind of literature new to the West, the literature of *fin' amors*: refined or courtly love.

Guilhem was born on October 22, 1071, the son of Guilhem the eighth Duke of Aquitaine and of Audiart, the young daughter of the Duke of Burgundy. His father died when he was fourteen, and at this young age he inherited lands which extended over an area a third the size of modern France. At this time he acquired the surname *lo Jovens* ("the Young"), a name by which he was known for the rest of his life. At first with the aid of his mother, then on his own, he was to rule these lands for forty-one years, occasionally trying to add to them at the expense of his neighbors.

When one considers Guilhem's poetry, one may find it hard to imagine that the span of his life coincides not with the rise of courtly literature in France but with the rise and dramatic spread of the *chansons de geste*. His character and career could hardly stand in more marked contrast to the martial, militantly Christian ethos of such a poem as the Oxford version of the *Chanson de Roland*, a poem which probably was composed not long after Guilhem succeeded his father to the duchy of Aquitaine. The extraordinary rise to popularity of these songs of heroism, sanctity, and sacrifice seems to have left no impression on the young Duke, to judge from his poetry. He had other concerns: lyric songs, love of women, and the extension of his frontiers through stratagem or warfare. The author of the thirteenth century *vida* (or capsule "life" of Guilhem) remembers him as both a gentleman and a rogue:

> The Count of Poitiers was one of the most courteous men in the world, and one of the greatest betrayers of women, and he was a good soldier at arms and ruled with a generous hand. He well knew how to compose songs and to sing. And he went through the world a long time tricking the ladies. And he had a son who took as wife the Duchess of Normandy, and their daughter was married to King Henry of England and was the mother of the young King [Henry II] and of Lord Richard [the Lion-Hearted] and of Count Geoffrey of Brittany.[1]

The information is incorrect, of course. No son of Guilhem married the Duchess of Normandy. To his son Guilhem X (1099–1137), however, was born a daughter Alienor (known to us today as Eleanor of Aquitaine), and this remarkable woman became Duchess of Normandy when she married Henry Plantagenet, the future King of England. The other information of the *vida* may be no more trustworthy, particularly the statement that Guilhem "went through the world for a long time tricking the ladies," a bit of information which may be based entirely on the farcical autobiography recounted in song 5 in this edition.

Through contemporary records and chronicles, a good deal more is known concerning Guilhem than can be learned from the impressionistic *vida*.[2] Probably the life of no other troubadour can be reconstructed in such detail. Altogether he emerges from history as a man of culture and intelligence, a proud man, neither exceptionally ruthless nor exceptionally heroic. For the most part he lived out his life during a time of peace and prosperity for the region of Poitou and Aquitaine. Despite the incessant petty war-making which was the bane of life throughout much of the Middle Ages, in retrospect the period of the eleventh and twelfth centuries takes on the aspect almost of a Golden Age for southwestern France. The Moslem threat of preceding centuries had been stopped on the other side of the Pyranees, while the war of northern France against southern France which is known as the Albigensian Crusade was not to cripple the region until the years 1208–1229. During Guilhem's lifetime the arts flourished in the neighborhood of Poitiers as in few other regions of Europe. Here would have been found little of the oriental splendor of such a city as Moslem Cordova, but on a more modest scale the city had its brilliance. Guilhem's realm was a rich one, and Poitiers was its jewel. Crowning the beauties of the city was the church of St. Hilaire, newly constructed under the patronage of Guilhem VIII and dedicated in May 1096. Guilhem's father was well known as a collector of manuscripts and as a patron of the Church, hence also a patron of the arts. We may imagine that in the arts, in letters, in statecraft, and in the craft of war the young Guilhem was given an education such as befitted his standing as heir to Aquitaine. His education must have been trilingual: Latin would have been the language of most of his formal schooling, *langue d'oïl* was his native tongue, and he proved himself adept in *langue d'oc*, the language of the south and the language in which his songs are composed. Guilhem's life is no rags-to-riches story. The young man would have grown up well groomed for the demanding life which awaited him upon the death of his father in 1086.

When Guilhem was nineteen he was married to Ermangarde, daughter of his father's perennial enemy Fulke, the fourth Count of Anjou. This frankly political attempt to patch up an ancient feud was unsuccessful, and within two years the marriage ended in divorce. Within another two years Guilhem arranged a more significant and lasting match with Philippa of Toulouse, widow of Sancho Ramirez, King of Navarre and Aragon, who had died earlier the same year in the siege of Huesca (1094). The haste with which Philippa remarried underscores the political nature of the match. Philippa was the daughter and the sole heir of William IV, Count of Toulouse. In the year 1088 William had departed for the Holy Land, leaving Toulouse in the hands of his brother Raymond of St.-Gilles. The marriage of Guilhem and Philippa can only have been undertaken in the hopes of uniting Toulouse and Aquitaine under the rule of a single couple, for Guilhem lost little time in moving against Raymond of St.-Gilles. In the summer of 1096, after Pope Urban II had stirred the hearts of men and women from all over Europe with his call for a holy crusade against the Turks, Raymond of St.-Gilles answered the call and left for the East at the head of a large army. Guilhem managed to restrain his crusading fervor, although Urban II had been his personal guest at Poitiers the preceding January. Instead he marched against

Toulouse and annexed it, possibly without opposition. Despite his plausible claim to the region, the Church threw its powerful weight against him. According to Papal policy, the Church served as guarantor of the lands of absent Crusaders. By moving against Raymond of St.-Gilles at this moment, Guilhem set himself on a collision course with the most powerful institution of his day and provided grounds for his eventual excommunication.

In 1101, perhaps encouraged by the success of the first crusaders in recapturing Jerusalem and in carving out kingdoms for themselves in the Mediterranean, Guilhem himself took up the cross and led a great army to the East. The expedition was a disaster from the start. In order to raise the vast sums of cash required for financing it, Guilhem sold his rights to Toulouse to Bertrand of Toulouse, son of Raymond of St.-Gilles. If he had hoped to recover Toulouse when he returned from the East in triumph, his hopes were to be disappointed. Of the great multitude who followed him from Aquitaine, most seem not to have returned. Many died in the course of the journey. Many more were cut to pieces by the Turks in a shocking slaughter in the wastes east of Byzantium. The Aquitanians' guide at the time of this slaughter was none other than Raymond of St.-Gilles, who by this time was a veteran crusader and who was chosen as guide specifically because he should have known how to choose safe routes. Was treason involved in Raymond's misguidance? Several of Guilhem's contemporaries thought so, but Guilhem himself seems to have come to Raymond's defense.[3] In any case, Guilhem and the remnants of his army spent a time licking their wounds under the hospitality of Tancred, King of Antioch, then arrived at Jerusalem in time to celebrate Easter. By the end of 1102 he was home in Poitiers.

The rest of Guilhem's life may be passed over more briefly. In 1108 King Phillip I of France died. Guilhem refused homage to his heir King Louis the Fat until Louis granted him weighty concessions. In 1109 Bertrand of Toulouse died, and within four years Guilhem occupied Toulouse for the second time and established his wife Philippa as sovereign. Whether because of this move against Toulouse, because of his marital infidelities, or because of the heavy hand which he may have put on the coffers of the Church, in 1113 Bishop Peter II of Poitiers proclaimed Guilhem's excommunication. In response, Guilhem placed Peter II under house arrest at the castle of Chauvigny, where he died two years later. By this time Guilhem was leading an openly adulterous life. While Philippa ruled over Toulouse, Guilhem remained in Poitiers in the company of his mistress the exotically named Dangereuse, also known as Maubergeonne, wife of the Viscount of Châtelleraut. Angered by Guilhem's open flaunting of the Church, Girard, Bishop of Angoulême, renewed his excommunication in emphatic terms. Soon thereafter Philippa retired from the world to seek comfort in the abbey of Fontevrault, where she died in 1117–1118. There she would have been the occasional companion of Guilhem's first wife Ermangarde of Anjou, who also had taken shelter at Fontevrault. One wonders what tales the two women may have exchanged, walking afternoons in the sunshine of the cloister.

With the death of Philippa, Guilhem no longer could maintain his claim to Toulouse, which eventually came under the rule of Alfonse-Jourdain, the young son of Raymond of St.-Gilles. In 1117 Guilhem's excommunication was lifted in exchange for concessions to the Church. In 1119–1120, whether in a new mood of piety or spurred on by the hope of material gain, Guilhem took up the cross again and led six hundred knights into Spain in aid of the crusade of King Alfonso of Aragon against the Almoravid Moors. Here he took part in the great victory of Cutanda. Upon his return to Poitiers he arranged the marriage of his eldest son, the future Guilhem X, to Aénor, the daughter of his mistress Maubergeonne by her husband Aimeric I of Châtellerault. Aénor soon gave birth to a daughter, Eleanor of

Aquitaine. Little is known of the last years of Guilhem's life. He died on Feburary 27, 1127,[4] at the age of fifty-four, and he was buried in Poitiers at the abbey church of Montierneuf.

If today we remember Guilhem as the apparent inventor of the code of *fin' amors*, his contemporaries admired him and reviled him for his outrageous sense of humor. One of the more lively anecdotes about him is told by William of Malmesbury:

> Near by a certain castle called Niort Guilhem built some little shelters that looked almost like monastic huts, and he raved that he was going to found an Abbey of Whores. And he sang that he was going to establish one woman or another (whom he named, all from famous brothels) as his abbess, his prioress, and his other officials.[5]

The story may be apocryphal, but it is in character. Guilhem rarely takes the stance of the deferential and long-suffering lover who sighs his way across the pages of a good deal of later courtly literature. As a man of wealth and standing, he seems to have been accustomed to speaking and acting as he pleased. In particular, Guilhem had good reason besides his excommunication to satirize the piety of people of the cloister. While he was away in Jerusalem, Philippa was gracious in her patronage of Robert d'Arbrissel, famed preacher and founder of the male-and-female abbey of Fontevrault. Robert had a way of attracting women by his preaching, particularly wealthy and attractive women of the upper class. Scurrilous tales were told about the nature of his devotions to the ladies. Guilhem could not have been pleased when Philippa retired to Fontevrault in 1116, thereby in effect surrendering the Toulousain to her husband's enemies. William of Malmesbury also related that Guilhem was so infatuated with a certain viscountess (doubtless his long-time mistress Maubergeonne of Châtelleraut) that he affixed a picture of her to his shield "so that he would support her in battle just as she supported him in bed."[6] Other chroniclers confirm this picture of Guilhem's impudence. Orderic Vitalis records that he was "overly facetious," although "bold and manly," and that he "surpassed even the comic entertainers in the multiplicity of his jests."[7] After his return from Jerusalem, Orderic adds, Guilhem "often recounted the miseries of his captivity in rhythmic verses with comic measures,"[8] but it is doubtful that Guilhem ever was taken captive during this campaign. Probably the author of the anonymous *Vita beati Bernardi abbatis de Tironio* summed up the attitude of many churchmen toward Guilhem when he called him simply "enemy of all shame and sanctity."[9]

UILHEM seems to have made no systematic effort to preserve his songs. Very likely he considered them the casual fruits of a few hours of leisure and pleasure stolen from a busy life. Only their continued popularity on the lips of others may have led to their being recorded in a number of thirteenth and fourteenth century *chansonniers*, long after they were composed. As one would expect, the songs vary from version to version, while the accurate definition of the canon of Guilhem's work has been a matter of dispute. "Farai chansonetta neuva" (song 8 in the Jeanroy edition), a poem long attributed to Guilhem, recently has been shown to be by a later hand.[10] It is omitted from the present edition. Its rejection from the canon renders obsolete a good deal of scholarship on the subject of Guilhem's place in the rise of the courtly love lyric, for the song in question goes farther in expressing a codified courtly view of love than does any other song attributed to him. Future scholars concerned with the origins and history of *fin' amours* no longer will be able to assume that the code of courtly love appeared on the scene already fully developed in the work of the first troubadour. A sharper distinction will have to be made between the art of Guilhem's songs—songs sometimes delicate, but more often outrageously comic—and the art of the songs of later troubadours.

NDERSTANDING the haphazard manner in which the songs came to be recorded, there is no way to establish their chronology or to decide whether or not they are representative of the larger body of poetry which Guilhem may have composed. Most modern editors have followed the convention of grouping the songs by theme: first the comic songs, then the serious love lyrics, and finally the single song of farewell. Such a grouping is as good as any, and for the sake of ease in cross-reference it is followed in this volume with one exception, the omission of the spurious song 8 and the renumbering of Jeanroy/Pasero songs 9-10-11 to be 8-9-10, respectively. One should bear in mind that this grouping of the songs is completely arbitrary. It offers no basis for the conclusion that Guilhem developed from a period of youthful levity, to a mature seriousness, to a final more somber wisdom. Any of these songs may have been composed at any time up to his dying day. There is no reason to suppose that Guilhem came to repent of his obscene songs. On the contrary, a case could be made that his burlesque songs express a more mature wisdom than do several of the serious love songs.

In reality, the songs might be grouped as efficiently according to their intended audience as according to their theme. The burlesque pieces (songs 1-3 and 5-6) clearly were intended for public performance before a group of men (*compaigno*). The effect of the songs would have depended on their manner of delivery before an audience of friends, very possibly noisy friends of the sort who are likely to have accompanied Guilhem on his frequent military expeditions. Although scarcely clerical in tone, these songs draw sustenance from the Medieval anti-feminist tradition. They tend to depict woman as a sexually voracious being who knows what she wants and who usually manages to get it. The punch of the humor of several of these songs comes when Guilhem names the real-life women whose adulterous appetites he has exposed so brilliantly. The serious love lyrics (songs 7-9) were composed for a particular woman, not necessarily the same woman in each case. Each reads as though it were composed for private performance before this woman. Each also presents the relationship between the lover and his lady in such general terms that the song could have been sung and enjoyed in public as well, whether by lovers or by connoisseurs of love poetry. These songs present the "new love" in pure form. They do so in a style suitable for mixed company. In two of these lyrics we see the *primavera* opening used for the first time in European vernacular poetry. In all three we see expressed the leading tenets of *fin' amors*: the ennobling power of love, the importance of secrecy, the duty of obedience on the part of the male lover, the exalted delight (*joi*) which is the reward of one who remains patient in the service of his beloved. One scarcely can imagine the horror that Ovid or Catullus would have felt in the face of the sentiment expressed in these pieces, yet these songs were to establish a convention of love which is still with us. For parallels to such an idealization of the beloved, one would have to look outside the realm of Latin letters to the love poetry of the Arabs and of Moslim Spain. But in Hispano-Arabic love poetry there is one difference: the lover and the beloved are both men.[11] Two songs stand alone. Song 4 ("Farai un vers de dreyt nien") is a mystery. It appears to have been composed for a particular friend, apparently an Angevin friend or fellow-singer who was skilled enough in song to be able to attempt to discover its "counterkey." Despite Guilhem's assertion that the song is not about love, the piece reads very much like a burlesque on the subject of the new love. Song 10 ("Pus de chantar m'es pres talenz") is the solemn song of farewell. It appears to have been composed as a public declaration, a sober settling of affairs on the eve of a real or metaphoric journey. The song would have been appropriate to any of several occasions in the author's life, including his severe illness during the years 1111–1112 and his expedition to Spain in the year 1119. To judge from the number of manuscript copies, this was the song by which he was known best. Here Guilhem addresses some of the same friends (*amics*) whom he addresses more familiarly in the burlesque songs, but the tone has changed. The laughter of his friends is stilled, and soon, Guilhem fears, his own voice will be stilled as well.

Such are the songs in brief. They are composed in a language which today is known either as *langue d'oc* (from "Oc," its word for "yes") or as Old Provençal (from *Provincia*, the former Roman territory of southern France, including an area far wider than modern Provence). It is not a dialect of French but is a language in its own right, closely related to Spanish, Catalan, and Italian. With regional variations, it was the language of common speech for persons who lived from the Limousin south to the Pyrenees and from the Atlantic Ocean east to the Côte d'Azur. The language of most troubadour poetry could be considered a literary *koiné* based on this speech. Guilhem himself refers to his language as *romans*, and in song 10 he distinguishes this tongue from the formal Latin of the Church.

In reading the songs in cold print, one should keep in mind that the text represents only one part of what once was a living fusion of words and melody. A large part of the original effect of the lyrics must vanish when we see them through the eye instead of hearing them through the ear. These songs were intended as performances, and without a living voice to perform them they come to us faintly. As Jaufre Rudel put the matter at the beginning of one of his songs, *No sap chantar qui so no di*: "One cannot sing who makes no sound, who gives no tune."[12] To one's vast regret, only a single fragment of the melodies of these songs has survived. The fragment is from the song of farewell (song 10), and it is transcribed as follows by Friedrich Gennrich:[13]

The rest of the melody is lacking. Presumably the person who noted the first bars thought that the remainder would be familiar to any reader. Such a practice of musical notation suggests that it was the tunes of these songs even more than their texts which led to their being remembered, much as today a number of popular songs soon would be forgotten if all that were known were their words.

A gap of a generation separates Guilhem from the next earliest troubadours whose works have come down to us, Marcabru (fl. 1129–1150) and Cercamon (fl. 1137–1152). Doubtless other persons were composing songs during this intervening period, notably Viscount Eble II of Ventadorn, a man so famed for his skills as to have acquired the name of "the Singer." If so, none of these songs has survived. In view of the isolated position of Guilhem at the head of troubadour tradition, one must be wary of ascribing to him the entire set of courtly attitudes which are associated with the work of his followers. One cannot be sure that he would have felt comfortable with all aspects of the art of love popularized by such a singer as Bernart de Ventadorn (fl. 1150–80) under the patronage of Eleanor of Aquitaine. Even less does his work correspond to the code of love which was drawn up by Andreas Capellanus at the direction of Marie de Champagne.[14] Guilhem's songs tend to be less analytic than later songs on the subject of love. His forms, like his jokes, are comparatively simple. In addition, even in his most refined love-lyrics he writes with a supreme self-confidence. Although appropriate to Guilhem, such self-confidence might have seemed mere arrogance in a poet of lower birth. Perhaps the quality which distinguishes his poetry most clearly from the poetry of other troubadours is its earthiness. Guilhem almost never idealizes the object of his love to the point of abstraction. Beneath the formal epithets of the courtly surface one perceives a flesh-and-blood woman, and one suspects that Guilhem honors this woman not because she denies her favors, but because he expects her to have the graciousness eventually to grant them. A frank sensuality stands at the core of his vision of life. The honest materialism of these songs distinguishes them immediately from the more delicate, more refined, and often more boring works of later troubadours. Even in the song of farewell (song 10) this materialistic note is heard like a refrain. This is no poem of renunciation, no *Busslied* (song of penance). It is a song of leave-taking, nothing more. Foremost in Guilhem's mind are the things which he must leave behind: his wide domains, the pride and chivalry of the court, the joys of love, his friends, even his robes. Like others of his songs, the piece ends not with blurry sentiment but with a concrete image, an image of the vair, gray, and sable furs which epitomize the quality of his life as Duke of Aquitaine and which he leaves now with a lingering backward glance.

If any two aspects of Guilhem's poetry stand out, they are first, this gravitation toward the concrete sensual image—vair fur, ponds without fish, horses, wine, the tumbling of dice, a warm fire, dinner with lots of pepper, a red cat, green fields, sunny clouds, a hawthorn branch trembling in rain and frost—and second, a corresponding gaiety of mood. *Joi* is a key word in his vocabulary, *joi* and its doublet *joven* (youth). One may search in vain in his songs for examples of philosophical discourse. The theme of death is absent save as a dark shadow in the last song. There is no autumn imagery, no winter imagery; there are no pictures of bereavement or cruelty, save for the burlesque cruelty of Lady Ermassen swinging the cat. God and His saints are often on Guilhem's lips, but as often in the comic songs as in the serious ones. To place Guilhem's poetry within the context of a Dark Age of drafty castles, overburdened peasants, and muttering beadsmen would be the utmost distortion. These songs show us the light side of the Middle Ages. Their cynicism blows like a fresh wind through an age of sometimes oppressive seriousness, as if in anticipation of the triumph of the comic muse in the work of Boccaccio and Chaucer.

Perhaps chiefly because of his gaiety, Guilhem has been characterized as an author without depth. "Guilhem's poems are light and charming, but they lack profundity." Thus Diez in 1882.[15] To put the matter thus is to put in negative terms what from a different point of view might be considered a virtue, or simply a feature of the man's style. Guilhem is a poet of the brilliant surface, not of the moody depths. He tends to see the various affairs of life—the various affairs of love in particular—as something to be enjoyed and perhaps laughed at, not as something to be lamented and endured. His gaiety is a positive force which is capable of transforming everyday matters into occasions for laughter and the appreciation of beauty. The utter lack of pretension of these songs sets them apart from the work of authors who too often seem unrelenting in the seriousness with which they take themselves and their art. For all of its gaiety, however, his poetry does not lack range. Guilhem composed not only some of the funniest of troubadour poetry but some of the most beautiful as well, including the stately "Ab la dolchor del temps novel," and his work is crowned by the sober song of farewell. Guilhem's genius was for the comic, but his talents did not stop there.

As the first and in certain respects the best of the troubadours, Guilhem IX occupies a special place in the history of lyric poetry in the Occident. "Everything that is commonly called poetry in the modern tongues may in some way or other trace its pedigree back to William of Poitiers." So W. P. Ker in his classic study *The Dark Ages*.[16] Ker may have been exaggerating to make a point, but he did so only slightly. Guilhem not only popularized a new style of poetry. He made popular a mode of thinking about reality—even perhaps a mode of experiencing reality—which previously was unknown in Europe north of the Pyranees. One cannot be sure that he was the inventor of the concept of *fin' amors*. Probably the roots of the concept extend in various directions, like the roots of any strong tree. The mystique of love appears to derive both from the realms of feudal and religious devotion and from the mystical love poetry of Moslem Spain and the Near East. The more cynical features of the comic songs can be traced back to Ovid and to other poets of Augustan Rome. In addition, very likely there existed a tradition of popular love-song in the south of France prior to Guilhem, a tradition which was not recorded because it lacked prestige. The law of *nihil ex nihilo*—nothing comes out of nothing—governs in literature as in life. All the same, a person who is familiar with the other literature of the period cannot fail to be struck by Guilhem's originality. Guilhem seems to have been that rare kind of human being who had the courage or the brashness to affirm the worth of certain kinds of human experience which before had attracted little attention. In comparison with him, many later troubadours seem slavish imitators. Like the majority of poets of any age, in the eyes of history they appear as derivative figures who spent their energies playing out variations on exhausted themes. For the most part Guilhem's songs are free both of the technical extravagance and of the sentimental excesses which mar the work of many of his successors, the unmistakable signs of a poetry in its decadence.

With the songs of Guilhem IX we see the first flowering of the art of the troubadours. What is perhaps most remarkable about this flowering is that in the course of almost nine centuries it has lost so little of its freshness. One need not approach these songs through a maze of interpretive scholarship. One need not painstakingly reconstruct their historical setting before one can appreciate their beauty or humor. Although certain inevitable obscurities cloud the texts, for the most part Guilhem's songs speak to us as clearly and directly as they did in their own time. In this way they fulfill the conditions of most great art. In reading these songs we know ourselves in the presence of a *maiestre certa*, an irrepressible master of songcraft, a man whom Ezra Pound fittingly has characterized as "the most modern of the troubadours."[17]

A note on the texts and translations. The translations are in accord with the teaching of St. Paul: "not of the letter but of the spirit; for the letter kills, but the spirit gives life." In newly editing the Old Provençal texts,[18] on the other hand, my guiding principle has been to keep as close to the manuscript reading as is possible within the limits of good sense. In cases in which a song is preserved in multiple versions, I have not tried to create a diplomatic text but have kept close to the readings of the version chosen as base text. So as to give the collection as much unity as possible, in the case of six of the ten songs I have chosen as base text *chansonnier* C (MS Bibliothèque Nationale fr. 856). This is a fourteenth century anthology attributed to the region of Narbonne. Several of its texts are shorter than those in the other manuscripts, but are artistically superior, and it is for aesthetic reasons rather than on the dubious grounds of greater or less authenticity that C has been preferred. For alternative texts, for a glossary, and for more detailed textual notes and commentaries than are included in the present volume, the reader is referred to the ambitious Italian edition by Nicolò Pasero.

Notes to the Introduction

1. Lo coms de Peitieus si fo uns dels maiors cortes del mon e dels maiors trichadors de dompnas, e bons cavalliers d'armas e larcs de dompneiar, e saup ben trobar e cantar. Et anet lonc temps per lo mon per enganar las domnas. Et ac un fill que ac per moiller la duquessa de Normandia, don ac una filla que fo moiller del rei Enric d'Engleterra, maire del rei Jove e d'en Richart e del comte Jaufre de Bretaingna. —*Chansonnier* I (MS Bibliothèque Nationale fr. 854), fol. 142a. Cf. Jean Boutière and A.-H. Schutz, *Biographies des troubadours* (Paris: Nizet, 1964), p. 7.

2. The following summary is based largely on the magisterial *Histoire des Comtes de Poitou, 778–1204*, by Alfred Richard, former Archivist of La Vienne (Paris: Picard, 1903), I, 382–506. On Guilhem's earlier years see further Léon Palustre, *Histoire de Guillaume IX dit le Troubadour, duc d'Aquitaine* (Paris: Champion, 1882.

3. See Richard, I, 435–436. In the spring of 1102, after the defeat of the French, Raymond fell into the hands of Tancred of Antioch, who imprisoned him under the charge that he had caused the defeat of the crusaders. Guilhem was one of a number of persons who secured Raymond's release.

4. The date of Guilhem's death is given as 1126 by those who follow the common medieval practice of dating the beginning of the year from Easter rather than from January 1.

5. Denique apud castellum quoddam, Niort, habitacula quaedam, quasi monasteriola, construens, abbatiam pellicum ibi se positurum delirabat; nuncupatim illam et illam, quaecunque famosioris prostibuli esset, abbatissam vel priorem, caeterasve officiales instituturum cantitans.—William of Malmesbury, *Gesta Regum Anglorum*, ed. Thomas D. Hardy (London, 1840), II, 670–671.

6. Legitima quoque uxore depulsa, vicecomitis cujusdam conjugem surripuit, quam adeo ardebat ut clypeo suo simulachrum mulierculae insereret; perinde dictitans se illam velle ferre in praelio, sicut illa portabat eum in triclinio. —*Ibid.*, II, 671.

7. Hic audax fuit et probus nimiumque iocundus, facetos etiam histriones facetiis superans multiplicibus. —Orderic Vitalis, *Historia AEcclesiastica* 10:20, ed. Marjorie Chibnall, V (Oxford: Oxford University Press, 1975), 324.

8. Miserias captiuitatis suae . . . multotiens retulit rithmicis uersibus cum facetis modulationibus. —*Ibid.* 10:21, ed. Chibnall, V, 342.

9. Totius pudicitiae ac sanctitatis inimicus. —Gaufridus Grossus, *Vita Beati Bernardi*, in J. P. Migne, ed., *Patrologiae Cursus Completus, Series Latina*, CLXXII (Paris, 1895), 1396.

10. See Angelo Monteverdi, "La 'chansoneta nueva' attribuita a Guglielmo d'Aquitania," *Siculorum Gymnasium*, n.s. 8 (1955), 6–15. Pasero relegates the song to an appendix, while Gerald A. Bond supports Monteverdi with additional arguments in his review article "Philological Comments on a New Edition of the First Troubadour," *Romance Philology*, 30 (1976), 344–345 (note 9).

11. An excursus here on the subject of the origin and history of *fin' amors* would go far beyond the intended scope of the present volume. The voluminous literature on the subject is reviewed with discretion by Roger Boase, *The Origin and Meaning of Courtly Love: A Critical Study of European Scholarship* (Totowa, N.J.: Rowman and Littlefield, 1977), especially chapter 3: "Theories on the Origin of Courtly Love" (pp. 62–99).

12. Song number 25 in Thomas G. Bergin, ed., *Anthology of the Provençal Troubadours*, 2nd edition revised and enlarged, Yale Romanic Studies, Second Series, 23 (New Haven: Yale University Press, 1973), I, 35–36.

13. Friedrich Gennrich, *Der musikalische Nachlass der Troubadours*, I (Darmstadt, 1960), 287. See the Jeanroy edition, p. 43, for a transcription by J. B. Beck which differs somewhat from the Gennrich transcription in its interpretation of the rhythm of bars 3 and 4.

14. See Andreas Capellanus, *The Art of Courtly Love*, trans. John Jay Parry (New York: Columbia University Press, 1941).

15. "Wilhelms Gedichte sind leicht und anmuthig, doch fehlt es an Tiefe." Friedrich Diez, *Leben und Werke der Troubadours*, 2nd edition, ed. Karl Bartsch (Leipzig: J. A. Barth, 1882), p. 5.

16. W. P. Ker, *The Dark Ages* (New York: Scribners, 1911), p. 6.

17. Ezra Pound, *The Spirit of Romance*, 2nd edition (New York: New Directions, 1952), p. 39.

18. I have consulted each MS in the original or in photocopy with the exception of *a* and V, for which I have relied on Pasero. The condition of V is too poor to yield a legible photocopy.

TEXTS AND TRANSLATION

Acknowledgment

Translations of songs 1-6 and 9 are included in the booklet *Seven Songs of Guilhem IX: First of the Known Troubadours* (Grilled Flowers Press: Tucson, Arizona, 1978). Previously several of these translations appeared in somewhat different form in the pages of *Arion, Kayak,* and *Occident*.

COMPANHO, FARAY UN VERS

Companho, faray un vers
    covinen
et aura·i mais de foudatz
    no·y a de sen
et er totz mesclatz d'amor   5
    e de joy e de joven.

E tenguatz lo per vilan
    qui no l'enten
o dins son cor voluntiers
    non l'apren.   10
Greu partir si fai d'amor
    qui la trob' a son talen.

Dos cavalhs ai a ma sselha
    ben e gen.
Bons son et adreg per armas   15
    e valen
e no·ls puesc amdos tener
    que l'us l'autre non cossen.

Si·ls pogues adomesjar
    a mon talen   20
ja no volgra alhors mudar
    mon guarnimen
que miels for' encavalguatz
    de nuill home viven.

FRIENDS, I'LL MAKE A SONG

Friends, I'll make a song
meant to please,
and it will be more full of fun
    than of good sense,
and it will be all a mix
    of love and joy and youth.

And you may take him for a churl
    who won't hear it
or take it willingly to heart.
But one who finds it to his taste
    will scarcely part from love.

I have two horses for my saddle
and they suit me fine.
Each one is a beauty: proud and bold
    and fit for arms,
but I can't keep both of them
    for neither one can stand the other.

If only I could keep the reins on them
    the way I'd like
I'd never have to rig my harness elsewhere.
I'd be better mounted
    than any man alive!

Laun fon dels montaniers   25
    lo plus corren.
Mas aitan fer' estranhez'
    ha longuamen
et es tan fers e salvatges
    que del bailar si defen.   30

L'autre fon noyritz sa jus
    part Cofolen
et anc no·n vis bellazor
    mon escien.
Aquest non er ja camjatz   35
    ni per aur ni per argen.

Qu'ie·l doney a son senhor
    polin payssen
pero si·m retinc ieu tan
    de covenen,   40
que s'ilh lo tenia un an
    qu'ieu lo tengues mais de cen.

Cavalliers, datz mi cosselh
    d'un pessamen.
Anc mays no fuy issarratz   45
    de cauzimen,
res non sai ab qual mi tengua,
    de n'Agnes o de n'Arsen!

The first is from the mountains.
She moves with the fastest.
But she's always been a shy one
    for the bit:
she's fierce, a wild one,
    and won't stay broken.

The other one grew up nearby
    near Confolens.
I doubt that I've ever seen a mount
    more beautiful.
I wouldn't trade her
for her weight in gold or silver.

When I gave her to her master
    she was a mere filly,
but I still keep a certain claim on her.
For every time he rides her
    I ride her a hundred.

Horsemen,
    help me out of this predicament!
I've never had a more difficult
    choice to make.
I don't know which mount to keep,
    Lady Agnes or Lady Arsen!

COMPAIGNO, NON PUS MUDAR

Compaigno, non pus mudar
    qu'eo no m'effrei
do novellas qu'ai auzidas
    et que vei
q'una domna s'es clamada   5
    de sos gardadors a mei.

[E] diz que non volo prendre
    dreit ni lei
ans la teno esserrada
    quada trei.   10
Tant l'us no·ill larga l'estaca
    que l'altre plus no la·ill plei.

Et aquill fan entre lor
    aital agrei:
l'us es compains gens <a foc   15
    manda carrei>
e meno trop maior nauta
    que la mainada del rei.

Et eu dic vos gardador
    e vos castei   20
e sera ben gran foli'
    a qui no·m crei:
greu verrez neguna garda
    que ad oras non sonei.

FRIENDS, I JUST CAN'T HELP

Friends, I just can't help being up in arms
    about the news I've heard.
A lady complains to me
    about her guardians.

She says that they will listen to no reason,
that there are three of them,
that they keep her locked up
    like some wild beast.
As soon as one loosens the tether
    there's another to pull it tight.

Their behavior is a constant nuisance
    and affront.
One of them puts on the airs of a gentleman
    . . . . .
and together they make a bigger racket
    than the king's entire household.

Gentlemen guardians:
I will put my cards on the table
and if you are smart
    you will pay attention.
Have you ever seen a watchdog
    who didn't at times
        doze off?

Qu'eu anc non vi nulla domn'   25
    ab tan gran fei
qui no vol prendre son plait
    o sa mercei
s'om la loigna de proessa
    que ab malvastatz non plaidei.   30

[E] si·l tenez a cartat
    lo bon conrei
adoba·s d'aquel que troba
    viron sei.
Si non pot aver caval   35
    [ela] cumpra palafrei.

Non i a negu de vos
    ja·m desautrei:
s'em li vedava vi fort
    per malavei   40
non begues enanz de l'aiga
    que·s laisses morir de sei.
Chascus beuri' ans de l'aiga
    que·s laises morir de ssei!

Frankly, I've never known a lady
(however impeccable her reputation)
who, if you denied her *every* plea,
    if you ignored her *every* cry for mercy,
if you cut her off from *all* respectable amusements,
    wouldn't take wicked measures.

If you deprive her of her customary wardrobe
won't she cover her nakedness
    with whatever comes to hand?
If she can't have a thoroughbred
    won't she settle for a mule?

No, there's not a man among you
    would deny it.
If a doctor proscribes strong spirits
    because you're ill
you'd drink water before you'd die of thirst.
Wouldn't any of you drink water
    rather than die of thirst?

COMPANHO, TANT AI AGUTZ

Companho, tant ai agutz
    d'avols conres
qu'ieu non puesc mudar no·n chan
    e que no·m pes.
Enpero no vueill c'om sapcha   5
    mon afar de maintas res.

E dirai vos m'entendensa
    de que es:
no m'azauta cons gardatz
    ni gorc ses peis   10
ni gabars de malvatz homes
    c'om de lors faitz non agues.

Senher Dieus quez es del mon
    capdels e reis
qui anc premiers gardet con   15
    com non esteis?
C'anc no fo mestiers ni garda
    c'a sidons estes sordeis.

Pero dirai vos de con
    cals es sa leis   20
com sel hom que mal n·a fait
    e peitz n·a pres:
si c'autra res en merma
    qui·n pana e cons en creis.

FRIENDS, I'M SO SICK AND TIRED

Friends, I'm so sick and tired
    of bad receptions
I can't help making a song about it.
All the same, I don't want to let the world
    in on the details.

Let me tell you in general
    how it stands.
I DON'T LIKE:
        1. guarded cunt.
        2. fishless ponds.
        3. boasts of men who don't deliver.

Lord God who art of the world
    Citadel and King,
why wasn't the first husband to hoard his cunt
blasted to dust?
All the same, there's never been a miser in this trade
    who didn't come off worse than his wife.

You see, I've developed a principle,
"The Law of Cunt" I call it
as a man who has done well by it
    and who also has come to know its sting:
JUST AS OTHER THINGS DIMINISH WHEN ONE TAKES
FROM THEM
    CUNT GROWS.

E sels qui no volra·n creire   25
　　mos casteis
an ho vezer pres lo bosc
　　en un deveis:
per un albre c'om hi tailla
　　en i naison dos ho treis.   30

E quan lo bocx es taillatz
　　nais plus espes
e·l senher no·n pert son comte
　　ni sos ses.
A revers planh hom la tala   35
　　si·l dampn[atges no·i a ges.]
Tortz es c'o [m planha la tala
　　quan negun] dan no·i a [ges.]

And if you don't want to believe me
go out and look in the woods
      in a tree-farm.
For every tree that's cut down
      two or three sprout in its place.

When the wood is thinned
      it grows back all the thicker.
The owner loses neither interest nor principal.
It would be right to regret the cutting
      if some loss were involved,
but only a fool regrets a bumper crop.

FARAI UN VERS DE DREYT NIEN

Farai un vers de dreyt nien.
Non er de mi ni d'autra gen
non er d'amor ni de joven
    ni de ren au,
qu'enans fo trobatz en durmen   5
    sobre chevau.

No sai en qual hora·m fuy natz.
No suy alegres ni iratz
no suy estrayns ni suy privatz
    ni no·n puesc au,   10
qu'enaissi fuy de nueitz fadatz
    sobr' un pueg au.

No sai qu'ora·m suy endurmitz
ni qu'ora·m velh s'om no m'o ditz.
Per pauc no m'es lo cor partiz   15
    d'un dol corau
e no m'o pretz una soritz
    per sanh Marsau!

Malautz suy e tremi murir
e ren no sai mas quan n'aug dir.   20
Metge querrai al mieu albir
    e no sai tau.
Bos metges es qui·m pot guerir,
    mas non, sia mau.

I'LL MAKE A SONG ABOUT NOTHING AT ALL

I'll make a song
        about nothing at all.
It won't be of love or of youth
or of anything else;
it's just something which came to me one day
        while I was dozing on horseback.

I don't know what star I was born under.
I'm neither happy nor sad,
        aloof nor friendly,
and I can't do a thing about it
for one night on a mountain
        someone put me under a spell.

I don't know whether I'm sleeping or waking
        unless people tell me.
My heart is split by grief
and to tell the truth
        I couldn't give a damn.

I'm sick, I tremble, I'm going to die
and I know no more about it than what I've heard say.
I'll go see a doctor
        but I don't know who.
He'll be a good one if he can cure me
        but a bad one if he can't.

M'amiqu' ai eu, no sai qui s'es,   25
qu'anc non la·n vi, si m'ajut fes.
Ni·m fes que·m plassa ni que·m pes
    ni no m'en cau,
qu'anc non ac Norman ni Frances
    dins mon ostau.   30

Anc non la vi et am la fort,
anc no·n aic dreyt ni no·m fes tort.
Quan non la vey be m'en deport,
    no·m pretz un jau,
qu'en sai gensor e bellazor   35
    e que mais vau.

Fag ai lo vers, no say de cuy,
e trametrai lo a selhuy
que lo·m trametra per autruy
    lay ves Anjau;   40
que·m tramezes del sieu estui
    la contraclau.

I have a lover
    but I don't know who.
To tell the truth I've never seen her.
If she's never pleased me
        at least she's never bothered me
and I couldn't care less,
for there's never been a Norman or a Frenchman
    in my house.

I've never seen her
    and I love her madly.
She's never treated me well or ill.
I'm perfectly happy not to see her,
        it's the same to me,
for I have another lover who's more beautiful
    and twice as rich.

That's it, that's my song
    whatever it's about.
I'll send it on
to one who will send it on
        down towards Anjou.
Let him, if he will, send back
    the key to its coffer.

EN ALVERNHE PART LEMOZI

En Alvernhe part Lemozi
m'en aniey totz sols a tapi.
Trobey la moler d'en Guari
    e d'en Bernart;
saluderon me francamen   5
    per sanh Launart.

Aujatz ieu que lur respozi.
Anc fer ni fust no·y mentaugi
mas que lur dis aital lati:
    "Tarrababart   10
marrababelio riben
    saramahart."

So dis n'Agnes e n'Ermessen
"Trobat avem qu'anam queren!
Alberguem lo tot plan e gen   15
    que ben es mutz
e ja per el nostre secret
    non er saubutz."

La una·m pres sotz so mantelh
et a mi fon mout bon e belh.   20
Meneron m'en a lur fornelh,
    e·l foc fo·m bo
et ieu calfei me voluntiers
    al gros carbo.

ONCE IN THE AUVERGNE, PAST LIMOUSIN

Once in the Auvergne, past Limousin
I was on the road incognito
and met with the wife of *en Guari*
    and she of *en Bernart*.
They greeted me openly
    in the name of St. Leonard

and here's now I replied.
No stammering, no twisting of words,
but I talked like this:
    "Tarrababart
marrababelio riben
    saramahart."

So Lady Agnes said to Lady Ermassen:
    "Just what we were looking for!
    Let's take him home.
    He's a mute,
    his tongue will never wag!"

So one took me under her cloak—
you know, I didn't mind—
and they took me to their fireside.
    The fire was lovely;
that was a treat, to warm my toes
    by the big coals.

A manjar me deron capos   25
e sapchatz ac i mais de dos
e·l pan fon cautz e·l vin fon bos
        e·l pebr' espes
e no·i ac cog ni cogastros
        mas sol nos tres.   30

"Sor, aquest hom es enginhos
e laissa son parlar per nos.
Aportatz lo nostre cat ros
        tost e corren
que li·n fara dir veritat   35
        si de res men."

Quant ieu vi vengut l'enujos
grans ac los pels, fers los guinhos.
Ges son solas no mi fon bos,
        totz m'espaven.   40
Ab pauc no perdiey mas amors
        e l'ardimen.

Quan aguem begut e manjat
despulley·m a lur voluntat.
Derreire m'aportero·l cat   45
        mal e fello
et escorgeron me del cap
        tro al talo.

Per la coa·l pres n'Ermessen
e tira el cat escoyssen;   50
plaguas me feyron mays de cen
        aquella ves.
Coc me mas ieu per tot aquo
        no·m mogui ges.

Then came dinner:
capons, and not just one or two,
hot bread, good wine,
    and plenty of pepper.
And no cook there, no kitchen help,
    just the three of us.

"Sister, the man's a fraud!
He's been playing dumb
to make fools of us.
Quick, get the red cat!
If he's been faking
that'll make him talk."

So they brought in the beast:
thick coat, fierce whiskers, and ugly as sin.
That was no laughing matter,
    I nearly fell over on the spot!
Right then I nearly lost my nerve
    and all the game.

When we had had enough to eat and drink
I undressed, as they wished.
But they came behind me
    with that damn cat:
he clawed me from my head
    down to my heel,

then Lady Ermassen took him by the tail
and started swinging.
That time I must have taken
    a hundred clawings.
It was pure hell, but through it all
    I never flinched.

Ni o feyra qui m'aucizes   55
entro que pro fotut agues
ambedos, qu'ayssi fon empres
    a mon talen.
Ans vuelc mais sufrir la dolor
    e·l greu turmen.   60

Aitan fotey cum auziretz:
C et quatre XX VIII vetz.
A pauc no·m rompet mos corretz
    e mos arnes
e venc m'en trop gran malaveg   65
    tal mal me fes.

Monet, tu m'iras al mati:
mo vers portaras el borssi
dreg a la molher d'en Guari
    e d'en Bernat   70
e diguas lor que per m'amor
    aucizo·l cat!

That cat nearly killed me, but I never struck him.
Never again do I wish to suffer
    pain like that!
I thought I'd wait until I'd fucked the ladies well,
both of them, which soon occurred
    just as I planned.

I fucked them as you will hear:
one hundred and eighty-eight times.
I nearly split my reins
    and the harness with them,
and I got the pox, too,
    it was that bad.

Monet, go thou tomorrow at matins.
Take my poem in your sack
and carry it right to the wife of *en Guari*
    and she of *en Bernart*
and tell them, for love of me,
    please drown that cat!

BEN VUELH QUE SAPCHON LI PLUZOR

Ben vuelh que sapchon li pluzor
d'est vers si's de bona color
qu'ieu ai trag de mon obrador,
qu'ieu port d'ayselh mestier la flor
    et es vertatz,   5
e puesc en trair lo vers auctor
    quant er lassatz.

Ieu conosc ben sen e folhor
e conosc anta et honor
et ai ardimen e paor;   10
e si·m partetz un juec d'amor
    no suy tan fatz
no·n sapcha triar lo melhor
    entre·ls malvatz.

Ieu conosc ben selh qui be·m di   15
e selh qui·m vol mal atressi
e conosc ben selhuy qui·m ri,
e selhs qui s'azauton de mi
    conosc assatz
qu'atressi dey voler lor fi   20
    e lor solatz.

Mas ben aya selh qui·m noyri!
Que tan bo mestier m'eschari
que anc a negu no·n falhi;
qu'ieu sai jogar sobre coyssi   25
    a totz tocatz.
Mais en say que nulh mo vezi
    qual que·m veiatz.

I'D LIKE EVERYONE TO KNOW

I'd like everyone to know
    if it's well made,
this song I've taken from my workshop;
for of this trade
      I bear the flower,
it's true, and for witness, when it's finished,
    I call the song itself.

Well do I know good sense from foolishness,
courage I know from cowardice,
    honor from shame,
and if you challenge me to a love-game
I can tell the poor job
    from the job done well.

Well do I know who speaks me well
    and who speaks ill.
I know when the joke's at my expense,
and if people enjoy my company
      I've enough sense
to wish them all prosperity.

Blessed be my parents!
For they've made me such a master in my trade
    I've never failed a soul.
When it comes to a game of chance
on the pillow, I know the winning rolls;
I'm good, best in the neighborhood,
      just as you see me now.

Dieus en lau e sanh Jolia
tant ai apres del juec doussa   30
que sobre totz n·ay bona ma.
E selh qui cosselh mi querra
    no·n l'er vedatz
ni un de mi no·n tornara
    descossellatz.   35

Qu'ieu ai nom "maiestre certa":
ja m'amigu' a nueg no m'aura
que no·m vuelh aver l'endema.
Qu'ieu suy d'aquest mestier, so·m va,
    tan ensenhatz   40
que be·n sai guazanhar mon pa
    en totz mercatz.

Pero no m'auzetz tan guabier
qu'ieu non fos rahuzatz l'autrier
que jogav' a un joc grossier,   45
que·m fon trop bos el cap primier
    tro fuy taulatz;
que·m guardiey no m'ac plus mestier
    si·m fon camjatz.

Mas elha·m dis un reprovier: 50
"Don, vostres datz son menudier
et ieu revit vos a doblier."
Dis ieu, "Qui·m dava Monpeslier
    non er laissatz."
E leviey un pauc son taulier   55
    ab ams mos bratz.

Et quan l'aic levat lo taulier
    empys los datz.
E·l duy foron cairavallier
    e·l terz plombatz   60
e fi·ls ben ferir al taulier
    e fo·m joguatz.

Praised be the Lord and St. Julian,
I've learned the rules of the game so well
    no one can boast a better hand than mine.
If anyone needs instruction in this sport
    I won't decline.
No one need turn from me
      disconsolate!

People call me "The Master Joiner."
Never has a girl employed me a night
    but she'll want me back the next.
For in this trade—
and I take pride in this—
      I'm so well versed
I can earn my bread in any market.

So don't make too much fun of me
    if I had a slight mishap the other day.
It was a game for big stakes.
I was doing fine in the opening games
      but when the moment came to cast
I looked about—the dice faltered—
    the game had altered.

So she said to me:
"My lord, thy cast is a bit light.
    I bid thee, cast again!"
Said I : "By Him who gave me Montpellier,
    I honor thy commands."
And I raised her game-board a little
      with my two hands.

And when I'd raised the board
    I took the dice.
      Twice
I shook them, and the third time
      CAST:
and they hit the game-board fast
    and the play was mine.

PUS VEZEM DE NOVELH FLORIR

Pus vezem de novelh florir
pratz e vergiers reverdezir
rius e fontanas esclarzir
    auras e vens
ben deu quascus lo joy jauzir   5
    don es jauzens.

D'amor non dey dire mas be.
Quar no·n ai ni petit ni re?
Quar ben leu plus no m'en cové;
    pero leumens   10
dona gran joy qui be manté
    los aizimens.

A totz jorns m'es pres enaissi:
qu'anc d'aquo qu'amiey non jauzi
ni o faray ni anc no fi.   15
    Qu'az esciens
fas mantas ves que·l cor me ditz
    tot es niens.

Per tal n'ai meyns de bon saber
quar vuelh so que no puesc aver.   20
E si·l reprovier me ditz ver
    certanamens:
a bon coratge bon poder
    qui·s ben sufrens.

NOW THAT THE FIELDS ARE GREEN AGAIN

Now that the fields are green again
the orchards
        flowering, rivers and streams
        flashing
and the winds soft,
well should each man enjoy
            what his heart desires.

Of Love
        let me breathe no word but good.
Yet why should I not enjoy his least favors?
Perhaps I deserve no else;
        yet easily
he grants great joy to those who observe
            his ordinances.

Day after day
it is the same with me:
        I have no solace of the one I love.
Thus was it always,
thus will it ever be.
Many a time the heart within me tells me
            "All is naught."

And this is the cause of my unhappiness:
I desire what I can never have.
Yet still no doubt
        the old saying speaks true:
"Everything comes to him who waits"
            if the heart be true.

Obediensa deu portar   25
a motas gens qui vol amar
e coven li que sapcha far
        faigz avinens
e que·s guart en cort de parlar
        vilanamens.   30

Del vers vos dic que mais en vau
qui ben l'enten e n·a plus lau
que·ls motz son fag tug per egau
        cominalmens
e·l son, et ieu mezeis lo·m lau,   35
        bos e valens.

Mon Esteve, mas ieu no·i vau,
        sia·l prezens
mos vers e vuelh que d'aquest lau
        sia guirens.   40

Those who wish to love
must be obedient,
and they should know how to perform
    acts which please,
and in court let them take good care
    not to speak like churls.

Concerning this song, let me say
it will be worth more to one who understands it
    and it will bring him praise.
The words are made all of a piece
    in harmony
and the melody, I believe I may say,
    a sheer delight.

Song, go thou to my Esteve
    for I go not.
Of my praise for thee
    be thou the proof!

MOUT JAUZENS ME PRENC EN AMAR

Mout jauzens me prenc en amar
un joy don plus mi vuelh aizir
e pus en joy vuelh revertir
ben dey si puesc al mielhs anar
quar mielhs onra·m, estiers cujar,   5
qu'om puesca vezer ni auzir.

Ieu, so sabetz, no·m dey gabar
ni de grans laus no·m say formir
mas si anc nulhs joys poc florir
aquest deu sobre totz granar   10
e part los autres esmerar
si cum sol brus jorns esclarzir.

Anc mais no poc hom faissonar
co's en voler ni en dezir
ni en pensar ni en cossir.   15
Aitals joys no pot par trobar,
e qui be·l volria lauzar
d'un an no·y poiri' avenir.

Totz joys li deu humiliar
e tota ricors obezir   20
midons per son belh aculhir
e per son belh plazent esguar
e deu hom mais cent ans durar
qui·l joy de s'amor pot sazir.

IN JOY I YIELD MYSELF TO LOVE

In joy
    I yield myself to love
as to a delight I prize above all else.
And since I would fain fall in love again
    meet is it that I love worthily,
for such a love would honor me
        more than all others known to man.

I am not one for boasting,
I know not of lush praise.
But if ever a joy could be brought to flower
    this could, and could
        shine
    among others
like the sun breaking through dark clouds.

Never could a man shape in his mind
    what this love is,
not in will nor desire,
thought nor dream,
    for this joy has no peer.
Would a man sing its praise aright
        he could not in a year.

Before this joy
        all other joys must bow,
all wealth and pomp submit
to my lady, for her graciousness
        and for the kindness of her eyes.
One who enjoys the favor of her love
will live to be past a hundred.

Per son joy pot malautz sanar   25
e per sa ira sas morir
e savis hom enfolezir
e belhs hom sa beutat mudar
e·l plus cortes vilanejar
e·l totz vilas encortezir.   30

Pus hom genser no·n pot trobar
ni huelhs vezer ni boca dir
a mos ops la·m vuelh retenir
per lo cor dedins refrescar
e per la carn renovellar   35
que no puesca envellezir.

Si·m vol midons s'amor donar
pres suy del penr' e del grazir
e del celar e del blandir
e dos sos plazers dir e far   40
e de son pretz tenir en car
e de son laus enavantir.

Ren per autruy non l'aus mandar
tal paor ay qu'ades s'azir
ni ieu mezeys, tan tem falhir,   45
no l'aus m'amor fort assemblar,
mas elha·m deu mo mielhs triar
pus sap qu'ab lieys ai a guerir.

Her love can heal the sick,
    her anger slay the healthy.
She can turn a wise man to a fool,
waste the beauty of the handsomest,
turn the noblest to a churl
       and ennoble the most vile.

Eyes cannot see nor lips describe
    one lovelier than she.
For my own self would I keep her
      that my heart be quickened
      and my flesh renewed
that it might never age.

Should my lady choose to grant her love
I would receive it
    give thanks
    and conceal and cherish it.
At her pleasure would I speak and act,
      her virtues celebrate
to the advancement of her praise.

By no other dare I send
    lest I offend,
nor do I dare sing out my love myself
I so fear ill success.
She must herself choose for the best:
      she knows
she is my only cure.

AB LA DOLCHOR DEL TEMPS NOVEL

Ab la dolchor del temps novel
foillo li bosc e li aucel
chanton chascus en lor lati
segon lo vers del novel chan;
adonc esta ben c'om s'aisi   5
d'acho dont hom a plus talan.

De lai don plus m'es bon e bel
non vei mesager ní sagel
per que mon cor non dorm ni ri
ni no m'aus traire adenan   10
tro que eu sacha ben la fi
s'el' es aissi com eu deman.

La nostr' amor va enaissi
com la branca de l'albespi
qu'esta sobre l'arbr' en treman   15
la nuoit ab la ploia ez al gel
tro l'endeman que·l sol s'espan
par la fueilla verz e·l ramel.

IN THE SERENITY OF EARLY SPRING

In the serenity of early spring
the trees leaf out
the small birds sing
            each
        in its own speech
            according voice to the new song:
so should each man delight
        in what he most desires.

And yet I see no sign, no messenger
        from where my thoughts most dwell
wherefore my heart
            darkens
        I cannot sleep, my steps
                falter . . .
I must have word
if her reply be as I ask.

Our love
            fares like the hawthorn branch
                tossed
                at clearing's edge
            night-
            long in rain
                    and frost
        till dawn when the sun's light
                    stain
                    -s the limbs and trembling foliage

Enquer me menbra d'un mati
que nos fezem de guera fi   20
e que·m donet un don tan gran,
sa drudari' e son anel:
enquer me lais Dieus viure tan
c'aia mas mans soz so mantel!

Qu'eu non ai soing d'estraing lati   25
que·m parta de mon Bon Vezi,
qu'eu sai de paraulas com van
ab un breu sermon que s'espel.
Que tal se van d'amor gaban;
nos n·avem lo pan e·l coultel.   30

I call to mind
　　　　one dawn:
we put an end to war,
she gave a gift
　　　　past price,
her own love and her ring . . .
God grant I live
　　　to have my hands beneath her cloak again!

I care not for their speech,
those who would plant strife
　　　　between my Good Neighbor and me.
I know words, how they go,
from small cause how they grow.
　　　Let others show
and vaunt their loves:
　　　　we have the bread, the knife.

POS DE CHANTAR M'ES PRES TALENZ

Pos de chantar m'es pres talenz
farai un vers don sui dolenz:
mais non serai obediens
en Peitau ni en Lemozi.

Qu'era m'en irai en eisil   5
en gran paor, en gran peril,
en guerra laisserai mon fil
e faran li mal siei vezin.

Lo departirs m'es attan greius
del seignorage de Peitieus;   10
en garda de Folcon d'Angieus
lais la terra e·l son cozi.

Si Folcos d'Angieus no·l socor
e·l reis de cui ieu tenc m'onor
faran li mal tut li plusor,   15
felon Gascon et Angevi.

Si ben non es savis ni pros
cant ieu serai partiz de vos
vias l'auran tornat en jos
car lo veiran jov' e mesqui.   20

Per merce prec mon compaignon
s'anc li fi tort q'il m'o perdon,
et ieu prec en Jezu del tron
en romans et en son latin:

WILL TO SONG SEIZES ME

Will to song seizes me:
I sing ill chance,
no more in Peitau nor in Lemozi
to join love's dance.

In danger, in fear
I set forth from this land.
My son I leave at war,
enemies at each hand.

Parting is hard
from the domain of Peitieus.
My son and lands I leave in the guard
of his cousin Fulke d'Angieus.

If Fulke guard him not well
(and the good King who grants my fiefs)
thieves will give him hell,
Gascons and Angevins.

Son, keep your wits.
You are yet young.
Let them not turn you to the streets
when I am gone.

My friends, *merci*:
my wrongs may you pardon me.
And I pray to Jesus of the Throne
in Latin and Occitan:

De proeza e de joi fui   25
mais ara partem ambedui
et eu irai m'en a scellui
on tut peccador troban fi.

Mout ai estat cuendes e gais
mas nostre Seigner no·l vol mais;   30
ar non puesc plus soffrir lo fais
tant soi aprochatz de la fi.

Tot ai guerpit cant amer sueill
cavalaria et orgoill,
e pos Dieu platz tot o acueill   35
e prec li que·m reteng am si.

Toz mos amics prec a la mort
qu'i vengan tut e m'onren fort
qu'eu ai avut joi e deport
loing e pres et en mon aizi.   40
Aissi guerpisc joi e deport
e vair e gris e sembeli.

Once friend to pride and mirth
I leave them both,
to Him set forth
who grants all sinners peace.

I have had joys in store.
Now our Lord wills it no more:
the weight has grown too much to bear,
the end so close.

I leave all I held dear,
all pride and chivalry.
It is the Lord's will, let it be
mine; may God receive me.

Friends, when I am dead
come by my bed,
do me all honor you are able.
Onetime joy filled my mind
night and day
abroad, at home, and by my table.
Now I leave joy behind,
vair fur, gray
and sable.

Textual Notes

Versions of Guilhem's songs are preserved in nine independent MSS, all of them *chansonniers* (or anthologies of lyric songs) which date from long after his death. To judge from variations which exist between versions of the same song, different *chansonniers* reflect different song traditions current in one or another part of Europe. The chief MSS fall into two groups, CE (from Languedoc) and DN (from Italy). The letter symbols by which the *chansonniers* are known were assigned by Karl Bartsch, *Grundriss zur Geschichte der provenzalischen Literatur* (Elberfed, 1872). For a description of the MSS see Alfred Jeanroy, *Bibliographie sommaire des chansonniers provençaux* (Paris, 1916; rpt. New York: Burt Franklin, 1971), and Clovis Brunel, *Bibliographie des manuscrits littéraires en ancien provençal*, Société de Publications Romanes et Françaises, 13 (Paris: Droz, 1935). The textual apparatus of the present edition has been kept to a minimum. Variant readings are cited only when the base MS has been emended or when the reading of the base MS is in doubt. The MSS:

C: Bibliothèque Nationale fr. 856 (Paris). 14th century, Languedoc.
D: Biblioteca Estense MS 45 (= α.R.4.4 Modena). 13th and 14th centuries, Italian.
E: Bibliothèque Nationale fr. 1749 (Paris). 14th century, Languedoc.
I: Bibliothèque Nationale fr. 854 (Paris). End of 13th century, Italian.
K: Bibliothèque Nationale fr. 22543 (Paris). 13th century, Italian.
N: Pierpont Morgan Library MS 819 (New York). Formerly Thirlestaine House MS 8335 (Cheltenham, collection T. Fitz-Roy Fenwick). 14th century, Italian. Double copies.
R: Bibliothèque Nationale fr. 22543 (Paris). Early 14th century, Languedoc.
V: Biblioteca Nazionale Marciana, app. cod. XI (Venice). 1268, Catalonian.
a: Biblioteca Estense MS Campori γ.N.8.4 (Modena). 16th century Italian copy of a late 13th century *chansonnier*.

1. COMPANHO, FARAY UN VERS
Texts: C 231a, E 115.
Base: C (Jeanroy C, Pasero E).
24 E; d'ome viven C. *27–28* tan fera estranheza longuamen C, aitan fera estranheza ha longuamen E. *30* ballar C, bailar E. *37* qu'ieu C, qu'ie·l E. *42* qu'ie·l tengues cen C, qu'ieu lo tengues mais de sen E.

2. COMPAIGNO, NON PUS MUDAR
Texts: N 229b–230a, N 234 ab (=N²).
Base: N (Jeanroy N², Pasero NN²).
1. Capital initials are lacking at the beginning of this and succeeding stanzas in both N and N². *2* auzidai NN². *16* mandatairei N². *21–22* folta qui NN². *28* mencei N, mercei N². *31* acarcat NN². *35–36* uver caval cumpra NN²; Pasero incorrectly reads compra. *42* que laisses N, que·s laisses N².

3. COMPANHO, TANT AI AGUTZ
Text: E 114–115.
15 Pasero incorrectly reads premier. *17* mestiero. *25* Pasero incorrectly reads sel. *29* n·i naison.

4. FARAI UN VERS DE DREYT NIEN
Texts: C 230b–231a, E 114.
Base: C (Jeanroy C, Pasero E).
5 fuy C, fo E. *7* guiza·m C, hora·m E. *13* fuy C, sui E. *22* tam C, tau E. *24* mas ja non C, mor non E. *39* trameta C, trametra E. *40* enves Peitau E. *41* estug C, escut E. *42* la soa clau E.

5. EN ALVERNHE PART LEMOZI
Texts: C 232ab, N 228ab, N 235 ab (=N²), V 148b.
Base: C (Jeanroy V, Pasero V). Jeanroy (pp. 34–36) and Pasero (pp. 133–135) give the reading of C in an appendix.
26 e sapchatz agui mais de dos V, e sazaz que foron mais de dos NN², line omitted C. *After 27* C adds et ieu dirney me volentos. *28* fort et espes C, e·l pebr' espes V, lo peure spes NN². *29* et anc sol no·y ac coguastro C, e no·i ac cog ni cogastros V, et non i fo cog ni cogastros NN². *30* mas quan nos tres C, mas sol nos tres V, sol que

nos tres NN². *34* Pasero incorrectly reads tuit. *43* Pasero incorrectly reads quant. *63* Pasero incorrectly reads ab pauc no·m rompei. *66* Pasero incorrectly reads tan.

6. BEN VUELH QUE SAPCHON LI PLUZOR

Texts: C 230b, D 198a, E 113–114, N 229ab, N 233b–234a (=N²).

Base: C (Jeanroy C, Pasero E).

25 que de jogar C, q'eu sai jogar D, qu'ieu sai joguar E, qu'eu sai jogar NN². *36* ai mo CNN², ai nom DE.

7. PUS VEZEM DE NOVELH FLORIR

Texts: C 231a–231b, E 115, *a* 459.

Base: C (Jeanroy C, Pasero E).

1 Pasero incorrectly reads novel. *17* res C, rens E. *18* tot niens C, tot es niens E*a*. *21*. e·l reprovier ditz ver C, aisel reprovers me ditz ver E, e sil te pro zi lei me diz ver *a*. *23* boder C, poder E*a*. *35* e·l sonet qu'ieu mezeis lo·m lau C, e·l son et ieu meteus m'en lau E, e·l sonetz ieu mezeis m'en lau *a*.

8. MOUT JAUZENS ME PRENC EN AMAR

Texts: C 230a, E 115–116.

Base: C (Jeanroy C, Pasero E).

5 orna·m CE. *14* con en C, cors en E. *33* la·n C, la E.

9. AB LA DOLCHOR DEL TEMPS NOVEL

Texts: N 228b–229a, N 235a (=N²), *a* 463, *a* 499 (=*a*²).

Base: N² (Jeanroy N², Pasero NN²).

1 capital initials are lacking at the beginning of this and succeeding stanzas in both N and N². *11* ben de fi N, tro qu'eu sacha ben de fi N². *15* trenan NN², treman *a*, tremblan *a*². *21* que·n NN², que·m *a*, qi *a*². *24* Pasero incorrectly reads son. *25* de lor lati NN², d'estraing lati *aa*². *27* pauralas N, paraulas (corrected from paurulas?) N², paraulas *aa*². *30* n·avem la pessa NN²*a*, n·aven lo pan *a*²; Pasero incorrectly reports coutel.

10. POS DE CHANTAR M'ES PRES TALENZ

Texts: C 230ab, D 190b, I 142b, K 128a, N 230a, N 234b–235a (=N²), R 8a, *a* 463.

Base: D (Jeanroy D, Pasero NN²).

6 en gran paor CKNN², en guerra et R, words omitted D. *10* Pasero incorrectly reads de for del. *17* Pasero incorrectly reads no for non. *21* cypaignon DI, companho C*a*, compaignon K, conpaigno N, conpaignon N², companhon R. *23* et il prec DIK, et ieu prec CR, et el prec NN²*a*. *40* et e D, et en CNN²*a*, et a IK, del R.

Commentary

1. COMPANHO, FARAY UN VERS. *Bibliography*: Charles Camproux, "Faray un vers tot convinen," in *Mélanges de langue et de littérature du Moyen Age et de la Renaissance offerts à Jean Frappier* (Geneva: Droz, 1970), vol. I, 159–172; Christopher Kertesz, "A Full Reading of Guillaume IX's 'Companho, faray un vers . . . convinen,'" *Romance Notes*, 12 (1971), 461–465; Judith M. Davis, "A Fuller Reading of Guillaume IX's 'Companho, faray un vers . . . covinen,'" *Romance Notes*, 16 (1975), 445–449. For most of eight stanzas Guilhem develops his predicament with mock seriousness. The punch comes only in the last line. The identity of the athletic ladies Agnes and Arsen is not known, but perhaps Agnes is to be identified with one of the heroines of song 5. Eight stanzas of three long lines each, divided usually 7 syllables plus 4, 7 plus 4, and 7 plus 7, with the rhyme on [ens] throughout. After stanza 8, E adds a *tornada* which is lacking in C:

> De Gimel ai lo castel
> e·l mandamen
> e per Niol fauc ergueill
> a tota gen
> c'ambedui me son jurat
> e plevit per sagramen.

> [Of Gimel I have the castle
> and the fief
> and Nieul makes me proud in the eyes
> of all the world,
> for both are mine by right
> and are pledged by solemn oath.]

Presumably the references are to the homes of the two ladies, Gimel in Corrèze and probably Nieul in Haute-Vienne. Guilhem takes as much pride in the high standing of the two ladies as he would take in the fine blood of a pair of thoroughbreds.

30. Literally "that she refuses to bear harness."

33. Co[n]folens: on the river Vienne northwest of Limoges. Davis ("A Fuller Reading," p. 448) would see in the place-name a "cheerfully obscene" pun.

41–42. Literally "for every year he keeps her, I keep her more than a hundred."

2. COMPAIGNO, NON PUS MUDAR. The range of metaphors in the song is characteristic of Guilhem: the tether, the watchdog, the wardrobe, the mule and the thoroughbred, and the clinching comparison of water vs. strong spirits. The form is the same as that of song 1, with the rhyme on [ei].

15–16. A *locus desperatus* which I have preferred to leave untranslated. Neither the reading *a foc manda carrei* of N nor the reading *a foc mandatairei* of N² is capable of easy interpretation. Jeanroy and Pasero emend *foc* to *for* and translate "courtois comme un charretier (?)," "gentile come un carrettiere." Bond ("Philological Comments," pp. 349–350), following Roncaglia, reads *foc* in the sense of "fire" and would relate *mandacarrei* to the root *manducare* "to eat." He sees the general sense of the lines as "their custom [*us*] is to sit around the fire and eat food."

27–28. Guilhem rings changes on the legal terminology of lines 5–8: *plait* "trial, case," *merci* "mercy, clemency," responding to earlier *clamar* "plead" and *dreit ni lei* "right nor law."

3. COMPANHO, TANT AI AGUTZ. *Bibliography*: Leo Pollman, "Companho, tant ai agutz d'avols conres," *Neophilologus*, 47 (1963), 24–34; Nicolò Pasero, "'Companho, tant ai agutz d'avols conres' di Guglielmo IX d'Aquitania e il tema dell'amore invincibile," *Cultura Neolatina*, 27 (1967), 19–29; Charles Camproux, "Seigneur Dieu qui es du monde tête et roi! (Canso III de Guilhem de Peitieus)," in *Mélanges de langue et de littérature médiévales offerts à Pierre Le Gentil* (Paris: S.E.D.E.S., 1973), pp. 161–174; François Zufferey, "Notes sur la pièce III de Guillaume de Poitiers," *Romania*, 97 (1976), 117–122. The situation is the familiar one of erotic misadventure—a woman, her lover, a jealous husband—but the working out of the theme is all Guilhem's own. The tone of the piece is detached, almost scientific. Guilhem has a lesson to expound, the "Law of Cunt," and he seems confident that the principle is powerful enough to sweep away all debate concerning the utility of a husband's setting a guard on his wife. The same form as in the preceding songs, with the rhyme on [es] or [eis].

15. Here and in lines 19 and 24, Pollman would deny the obscene meaning of the word *cons* and would render the word as "married woman." As a consequence, he sees the meaning of stanza 4 as "very obscure." The present generally-accepted interpretation seems both more clear and more natural. For a parallel to Guilhem's placing an obscenity at the very center of the piece, see Guerin's fabliau "Du chevalier qui fit les cons parler" ("The Chevalier Who Made Cunts Talk"), in Robert Harrison, *Gallic Salt: Eighteen Fabliaux Translated From the Old French* (Berkeley: University of California Press, 1974), pp. 218–255.

33–34. Literally "and the owner loses neither his count (account?) nor his sense."

36–38. Certain words have been lost by the removal of an illumination from the opposite side of the folio. The present reconstruction differs from that advanced by Zufferey ("Notes," p. 120) only by the reading *a* in place of *es* in line 36 and by the reading *quan* in place of *si* in line 38.

4. FARAY UN VERS DE DREYT NIEN. *Bibliography*: Erich Köhler, "'No-sai-qui-s'es—No-sai-que-s'es' (Wilhelm IX von Poitiers und Raimbaut von Orange," in *Mélanges de linguistique romane et de philologie médiévale offerts à M. Maurice Delbouille* (Gembloux: Duculot, 1964), vol. II, 349–366; Lynne Lawner, "Notes Towards an Interpretation of the 'vers de dreyt nien,'" *Cultura Neolatina*, 28 (1968), 147–164; Lawner, "'Norman ni Frances,'" *Cultura Neolatina*, 30 (1970), 223–232; Lawner, "'Tot es niens,'" *Cultura Neolatina*, 31 (1971), 155–170; Dietmar Reiger, *Der vers de dreyt nien Wilhelms IX. von Aquitanien: Rätselhaftes Gedicht oder Rätselgedicht?* (Heidelberg: Winter, 1975); Charles Camproux, rev. of Reiger, *Revue des langues romanes*, 82 (1976), 251–258. The most enigmatic of Guilhem's songs, apparently deliberately so. Despite the author's claim that the song is about nothing at all, commentators have searched diligently and sometimes ingeniously for a supposed solution to the work, a special "counterkey" that will unlock its secrets. The commonly accepted solution is love, even though Guilhem flatly declares that the song is not about love. Despite Guilhem's protestation, much of the song reads like a burlesque on the subject of the love-sickness suffered by devotees of the "new love." If so, the song presupposes a strong tradition of courtly love-lyric by the time of Guilhem.

7. Literally "in what hour" (*hora*). Cf. modern English *horoscope*.

17. Literally "I don't care a mouse about it."

18. St. Martial: celebrated patron of the Limousin, in particular of the monastery of St. Martial in Limoges.

36–37. Between stanzas 6 and 7, C lacks a stanza which reads as follows in E:

No sai lo luec ves on s'esta
si es en pueg ho en pla.
Non aus dire lo tort que m'a,
    abans m'en cau.
E peza·m be quar sai remanc
    [ab] aitan vau.

[I don't know where she lives,
on a mountain or in the plains.

> I don't dare tell how she wrongs me,
> I hardly care.
> And since I don't like staying here
> I'll take my leave.]

Pasero incorrectly reads *rema* in the next to the last line.

5. EN ALVERNHE PART LEMOZI. *Bibliography*: István Frank, "Babariol-babarian dans Guillaume IX," *Romania*, 73 (1952), 227–234; A. Del Monte, "En durmen sobre chevau," *Filologia romanza*, 2 (1955), 140–147; J. Monfrin, "Ne savoir ne bu ne ba," *Romania*, 78 (1957), 98–100; Erich Köhler, "Wilhelm IX, der Pilger und die rote Katze," in *Mélanges de langue et de littérature médiévales offerts à Pierre Le Gentil* (Paris: S.E.D.E.S., 1973), pp. 421–434; Alan R. Press, "Quelques observations sur la chanson V de Guillaume IX: 'Farai un vers pos mi sonelh,'" in *Études de civilisation médiévale (IXe-XIIe siècles): Mélanges offerts à Edmond-René Labande* (Poitiers: C.E.S.C.M., 1975), pp. 603–609. The most famous of the burlesque songs and one of the finest comic narrative poems of any time. The details are especially fine: the warm reception under the lady's cloak, the comfortable fire, the abundance of pepper. Somehow it seems necessary that the cat be *red*. Also fine is the poetic justice of the piece. The cat gives Guilhem more than a hundred stripes; Guilhem later returns more than a hundred blows of his own. The ladies welcome the wanderer because they believe he is mute. The song itself—sung on the lips of how many?—is his proof to the contrary. Boccaccio takes up the theme of the song again at far greater length in his *Decameron*, 3:1.

The base MS of the present edition, C, lacks two introductory stanzas which are found in the other MSS. The reading of V:

> Farai un vers pos mi sonelh
> e·m [MS en] vau e m'estauc al solelh.
> Donnas i a de mal conselh
>   et sai [dir] cals:
> cellas c'amor de cavalier
>   tornon a mals.

> Dona fai pechat mortal
> qe non ama cavalier leal
> mais aman monges et clersgau.
>   Non a raizo;
> per dreg la deuria hom cremar
>   ab un tezo.

> [I'll make a song since I'm drowsy
> as I ride along in the sun.
> Some women are wicked schemers
>   and I can say who:
> those who would spurn the love
>   of an honest knight.

> Women commit a mortal sin
> who scorn the love of a faithful knight
> and couple with monks and clerks.
>   It's just not right;
> such women deserve to be burnt alive
>   at the stake.]

An additional stanza is lacking in C between stanzas 1 and 2. The reading of N:

> Una mi dis en son latin:
> "Et Deus te salve, don pelegrin!
> Molt me pari de bel eisin
>   men esient;
> mais trop en vai per sto camin
>   de folla gent."

> [One of them said to me in her argot:
> "God save you, worthy pilgrim!
> You seem to be a good sort,
>   I would say,
> but a lot of witless persons
>   pass this way."]

Pasero incorrectly reports *Deu* in the second line. Although probably authentic, the three stanzas add little to the piece, which moves at a more effective pace in C. They may have been omitted by an intelligent scribe.

   2. *A tapi*: probably "in disguise," specifically in a pilgrim's coarse garb.

   3–4. *En Guari, en Bernart*: "Lord Guari, Lord Bernart" (*en* from Latin *dominus*, analagous to Spanish *Don*). It is important (a) that the ladies be of high degree, (b) that they be married, and (c) that their husbands be named explicitly. Part of the humor of the piece depends on the audience's recognition that these are real-life ladies rather than stock characters out of a fabliau. Again at the end of the song (lines 69–70) Guilhem makes a point of referring to the husbands specifically by name.

   6. St. Leonard: a hermit saint of sixth century Limousin who gave his name to St. Léonard de Noblat in Haute-Vienne.

   8. *mentaugi*: Pasero incorrectly reads *mentagui*, Jeanroy *mentaugui*. The line translates literally "I didn't talk falsely about iron or wood," "about tool or handle." Apparently an idiom for "I didn't beat around the bush."

   10–12. NN² read simply *babariol babariol babarian*. The reading of C would appear to be closer to the original. Could it be that Guilhem is speaking Arabic to the ladies, as Nykl and Briffault have claimed, even obscene Arabic, as has been supposed by Lévi-Provençal? See Pasero, pp. 145–146, for their proposed reconstructions of the passage. If this interpretation is correct, then the Arabic came to be garbled almost beyond recognition in the course of the song's transmission. On the other hand, István Frank ("Babariol-babarian") takes the original passage to have been nonsense syllables and would deny any special authority to C. He sees no Arabic element in the song. Whatever the original reading, the scribe of C is likely to have taken the words simply as nonsensical babbling.

   55–60. V gives the following stanza in place of stanza 10 of C:

> "Sor," diz n'Agnes a n'Ermessen,
> "mutz es, qe ben es connoissen;
> sor del banh nos apareillem
>   e del sojorn."
> Ueit jorns ez encar mais estei
>   en aquel forn [MS torn].

> "Sister," said Agnes to Ermassen,
> "he's mute, it's perfectly clear.
> Let's get ready for the bath

> and for some fun."
> Eight days and more I stayed
> in that oven.

In the last line, Jeanroy's emendation of *torn* "neighborhood" or perhaps "tower" to *forn* "furnace, heated room" fits with the *fornelh* of line 21 and leads to a good joke, but is rejected by Pasero (p. 154) and Bond ("Philological Comments," p. 354). Nichols, in *L'Esprit créateur*, 16 (1976), pp. 23–24, note 9, favors the emendation.

67. Monet: Guilhem's *jongleur*. As a man of wealth, Guilhem can afford to have a hired singer perform his songs.

6. BEN VUELH QUE SAPCHON LI PLUZOR. Like song 1, an exercise in *double entendre*, but here the weave of double meanings is far more artful. The key term is *mestiers*, "occupation" or "trade." With typical modesty, Guilhem claims that in his *mestiers* he is a master craftsman (*maiestre certa*). The joke is that his trade turns out to be not only songcraft but lovecraft, and in each field he claims pre-eminence. If we are to take seriously Guilhem's reference to the *mestiers* of song-writing, then Guilhem appears to have thought of himself as working in a well-established tradition of vernacular poetry. Technically a *tour de force*: short lines ending always in [atz] punctuate stanzas which are built up of five long lines ending on [or] for two stanzas, then on [i], then [a], then [ier], with a six-line *tornada* at the end.

2. Color: one is intended to think of the "colors" of medieval rhetoric, but the sense of "trick" may be present beneath the surface.

29. St. Julian, patron of hospitality.

53. Montpellier: the Church would have taken issue with Guilhem's claim of divine blessing for his annexation of the city.

59–60. The lines are difficult to interpret, but the literal sense appears to be "and two went tumbling (?) and the third plunged." If this is Guilhem's intention, the metaphor is more graphic than is suggested by the present non-literal paraphrase. See Bond, p. 357, for an alternative suggestion.

7. PUS VEZEM DE NOVELH FLORIR. One of the loveliest of Guilhem's lyrics and his most explicit testament of love. Here we see the *primavera* opening which was to become a commonplace of troubadour poetry. The fields are green, the streams are flashing with spring floodwaters—it is the time for lovers to rejoice. Here also we see the typically unsatisfied lover of troubadour tradition: patient, somewhat bewildered, long-suffering. Within this setting, evidently already conventional in Guilhem's day, the author enters upon a thoughtful discourse on the subject of love and its *aizimens* ("rules," "commandments"). In keeping with these rules, it is the lady who has the power to grant or to withhold favors. The lover has only the power to wait. The more worthy the object of his love, the longer he deserves to wait. He could have set his desire on a milkmaid, after all, but if he had done so he could have expected mere sensual pleasure and not the exalted joy which is the reward of the patient devotee of *fin' amors*. Between stanzas 4 and 5, C lacks a stanza which is present in the other versions. The reading of E:

> Ja no cera nuils hom ben fis
> contr' amor si non l'es aclis
> et als estranhs et als vezis
>   non es consens,
> et a totz sels d'aicel aizi[s]
>   obediens.

[One who would serve Love faithfully
must humble himself;
he must act courteously
    to strangers and to friends alike,
and he must bow his will
    to all members of his lady's household.]

Pasero incorrectly reads *sera* in the first line, *aicels* in the last. The key terms of the code are drawn from the worlds of feudal service and religious submission: *fis* "faithful," *aclis* "humble," *consens* "agreeable," *obediens* "obedient." To judge from the extent to which it advances a fully codified doctrine of love, the stanza appears to derive from a time later than Guilhem.

11. be: Pasero reports *be·n*, but there is no mark of abbreviation over MS *e*.

23-24. The proverb is international in currency: for examples see Jerzy Gluski, *Proverbs: A Comparative Book of English, French, German, Italian, Spanish, and Russian Proverbs with a Latin Appendix* (Amsterdam: Elsevier Publishing Company, 1971), p. 205.

37. Esteve: a *senhal* (pseudonym, code name) for the lady. The other MSS give more precise information than C concerning the lady's dwellingplace. The double *tornada* of E:

A Narbona, mas ieu no·i vau
    sia·l prezens
[mos vers] e vueill que d'aquest lau
    me sia guirens.
Mon Esteve, mas ieu no·i vau,
    sia·l prezens
mos vers e vueill que d'aquest lau [MS vers]
    sia guirens.

[At Narbonne—for I go not—
    may my song be presented,
and I would that of my praise for it
    it be the proof.
To my Esteve—for I go not—
    may my song be presented,
and I would that of my praise for it
    it be the proof.]

8. MOUT JAUZENS ME PRENC EN AMAR. Jeanroy/Pasero no. 9. If Guilhem is to be considered a "trovatore bifronte," in the terms of Pio Rajna, then this song epitomizes his courtly face. Here is the new love at its most pure. Technically the song is another *tour de force*: eight stanzas of seven long lines each, each stanza with the same rhyme scheme based on the two homophonous rhymes [ar] and [ir]. Almost all the rhyming words are verbs. The key verb is saved until the end: *guarir* "to heal, to cure."

37. Midons: literally "my lord," not "my lady" (*madompna*). The custom of referring to the beloved as if she were a man appears to derive from Arabic tradition.

9. *AB LA DOLCHOR DEL TEMPS NOVEL*. Jeanroy/Pasero no. 10. *Bibliography*: D. Woll, "Zu Wilhelms IX. Kanzone 'Ab la dolchor del temps novel,'" *Archiv für das Studium der neueren Sprachen und Literaturen*, 117 (1966), 186–188; George Economou, "Test of Translation X: Guillem Comte de Peitau's 'Ab La Dolchor Del Temps Novel,'"*Caterpillar*, 10 (January 1970), 150–158; Antoinette Knapton, "Un Poème Incantatoire de Guillaume IX," *Revue du Pacifique*, 1 (1975), 87–94. A lyric worthy to be set beside the finest love poems of any

time, from Sappho to W. C. Williams. It unfolds in a stately progression: the vernal opening, the lover's disquietude, the simile of the hawthorn branch, the journey into memory, the final awareness of self-sufficiency in love. Here as elsewhere in Guilhem's songs the speaker speaks with confidence. Here is no pale, fainting lover of later courtly or Petrarchan tradition. Guilhem knows exactly what he wants, and despite temporary setbacks he expects to get it. In the same manner, the object of his love is no idealized phantom. She is a sensual being, like the women of the burlesque poems. Unlike them, she commands the utmost repect. She and her lover may be separated, but when they are together there exist no barriers of pretense between them: *we have the bread, the knife*. Formally a more varied piece than the preceding one thanks to the counterpoint among the three rhymes [el], [i], and [an].

9. Mos cors: probably not "my heart," despite the present translation, but simply "I" (cf. Latin *corpus meus*).

22. As opposed to *fin' amors*, *drudaria* implies a sensual relationship. As in the modern wedding ceremony, the gift of the ring may represent both fidelity and the surrender of virginity.

25–28. A reference to the scandalmongers (*losengiers*) who are ever ready to prey on unwary lovers.

26. Bon Vezi: another *senhal* for the lady.

10. PUS DE CHANTAR M'ES PRES TALENZ. Jeanroy/Pasero no. 11. *Bibliography*: J. Storost, "'Pos de chantar m'es pres talenz': Deutung und Datierung des Bussliedes des Grafen von Poitiers," *Zeitschrift für französische Sprache und Literatur*, 63 (1940), 356–368; Aurelio Roncaglia, "'Obediens,'" in *Mélanges de linguistique romane et de philologie médiévale offerts à M. Maurice Delbouille* (Gembloux: Duculot, 1964), vol. II, 597–614. The song cannot be dated with certainty, but it reads as a solemn farewell to Guilhem's native Aquitaine and to its pleasures. Although some scholars would read the piece as a song of repentence, the mood of regret is tempered by the speaker's evident love for the material things which he must leave behind. To judge from lines 31–32 and 37, the speaker is no longer a young man. The song is not likely to have been composed on Guilhem's death bed, however, for his son is said to be still young, and in 1127 his son was 28 years old. A date during the second decade of the twelfth century seems likely. If Storost is correct, the piece was composed during the years 1111–1112, when Guilhem suffered a severe illness. Whatever the date and circumstances of composition of the song, it stands out among extant troubadour poetry for its stark dignity. Here we see the plain style—*trobar plan*—at its best. The simple stanzaic form contributes to the sense of grace. The order of the stanzas is preserved differently in the different manuscripts. Although each order is coherent, that of the group to which D belongs is best.

D,I,K,N,N²	1	2	3	4	5	6	7	8	9	10	11
C	1	3	4	2	5	7	9	–	6	10	11
R	1	9	3	4	–	2	6–10	7	–		

I and K lack stanza 6, N lacks stanza 11, and N² lacks stanza 8.

12. Folcon d'Angieus: not Guilhem's contemporary Fulke IV, Count of Anjou (d. 1109), but his son Fulke V, Count of Anjou from 1109 to 1129. Fulke V was the third cousin of Guilhem X and was his elder by several years, thus he could have acted as his guardian. Guilhem X seems to have weathered the storm of his father's absence without serious mishap. He assumed his father's titles upon Guilhem's death in 1127. He died in April, 1137, on the pilgrimage route to Compostella. The troubadour Cercamon composed a *planh* (lament) for his death, the earliest recorded example of the genre: the text is given in the Bergin anthology, vol. I, 29–30.

14. E·l reis: King Louis VI of France. The line may be taken not simply as a statement of fact, but as a compliment addressed to a man whom Guilhem rivalled in power.

24. En romans et en son latin. In what appears to be a bit of playfulness breaking through the solemn surface of the song, Guilhem contrasts his own native speech (*romans*) with Jesus' tongue (*son latin*), the Latin of the Church.

37. Amics: here probably not only "friends" but "vassals."

42. Vair e gris: according to Bond ("Philological Comments," p. 360), the two paired terms serve to describe "the variegated shine of squirrel fur." Probably the allusion is not only to precious furs in general, but to Guilhem's ducal robes.

LIST OF POEMS

Note on Pronunciation

Troubadour songs were composed for the ear, not for the eye. Although the tunes of many songs have been lost, there is no reason for a reader to be deprived of the pleasure of hearing at least part of their verbal music. The exact pronunciation of *langue d'oc* is a matter of debate, but the reader who knows little or none of the language might take the following as rules of thumb.

1. Give vowels their usual Continental values as in modern French, Spanish or Italian.

2. Pronounce all consonants. There are no silent letters except in the case of an elided vowel.

3. Avoid the nasalization of vowels which has become a prominent feature of modern French.

In addition, several features of the language are worthy of special note.

4. The consonants *c* and *g* are pronounced as hard (k) and (g) before back vowels (*cor, caval; gardadors, guarnimen*). Before front vowels they are pronounced as the affricates (ts) and (j), respectively (*cen, certa; gen, qel*).

5. The consonant *z* is pronounced (ts): *bellazor, Lemozi*.

6. The digraphs *nh, gn,* and *ng* all are pronounced like the *ñ* of Spanish *señor: senher, seignoratge, companho, compaigno, soing*.

7. The digraphs *lh* and *ll* represent a palatalized *y* sound as in the *ll* of modern French *brilliant: somelh, falhi, orgoill, foillo*. Approximately the same sound may be represented by the letter *j* between vowels: *aja, ploja*.

8. The raised dot between letters is purely typographical. It has no effect on pronunciation and it does not appear in the MSS. In modern editions it serves visually to distinguish the word *non* from the contraction no·n (= *no* + *en*), for example.

191

Select Bibliography

For a comprehensive bibliography the reader is referred to Martín de Riquer's
Los Trovadores: Historia, literaria, y textos.

MUSICAL

Apel, Willi. *The Notation of Polyphonic Music, 900–1600*. 5th edition. Cambridge, Mass., 1953.

Aubry, Pierre. *Cent motets du XIIIe siècle, publiés d'après le manuscrit Ed. IV. 6 de Bamberg*. 3 vols. Paris, 1908, rpt. New York, 1964.

Aubry, P. *Le Roman de Fauvel: Reproduction phototypique du manuscrit français 146 de la Bibliothèque Nationale de Paris*. Paris, 1907.

Aubry, P. *La Rhythmique musicale des troubadours et des trouvères*. Paris: Champion, 1907.

Aubry, P. "L'Oeuvre mélodique des troubadours et des trouvères," *Revue Musicale*, 7 (1907), pp. 317–332, 347–360, 389–395.

Beck, Jean Baptiste. "Der Takt in den Musikaufzeichnungen des XII. und XIII. Jahrhunderts," *Riemann-Festschrift: Gesammelte Studien*. Leipzig: M. Hesse (1909), pp. 166–184.

Beck, J. B. *Die Melodien der Troubadours*. Strassburg: K. J. Trübner, 1908.

Beck, J. B. "Die modale Interpretation der mittelalterlichen Melodien," *Caecilia* (1907), pp. 97ff. (1908), pp. 71ff.

Beck, J. B. *Les Chansonniers des troubadours et des trouvères*. no. 1: *Le Chansonnier Cangé*. 2 vols. Philadelphia: University of Pennsylvania Press, 1927. no. 2: *Le Manuscrit du Roi*. 2 vols. Philadelphia: University of Pennsylvania Press, 1938.

Beck, J. B. "Zur Aufstellung der modaler Interpretation der Troubadoursmelodien," *Sammelbände der Internationalen Musikgesellschaft*, 12 (1910–1911), pp. 316–324.

Boogaard, Nico J. H. van den. *Rondeaux et refrains du XIIe siècle au début du XIVe*. Paris: Klincksieck, 1969.

Chailley, Jacques. "Quel est l'auteur de la 'théorie modale' dite de Beck-Aubry?," *Archiv für Musikwissenschaft*, 10 (1953), pp. 213–222.

Coussemaker, Charles Edmond Henri de. *L'Art harmonique aux XIIe et XIIIe siècles*. Paris, 1865.

Coussemaker, C. E. H. de. *Histoire de l'harmonie au Moyen Age*. Paris, 1852.

Coussemaker, C. E. H. de. *Scriptorum de musica medii aevi novam seriem*. 4 vols. Paris, 1864–1876.

Crocker, Richard L. *The Early Medieval Sequence*. Berkeley, 1977.

Davison, Archibald T. and Willi Apel (eds.). *Historical Anthology of Music*. Vol. 1. Revised edition. Cambridge: Harvard University Press, 1964, pp. 14–21.

Evans, Paul. *The Early Trope Repertory of Saint Martial de Limoges*. Princeton Studies in Music, II. Princeton, 1970.

Gennrich, Friedrich. "Grundsätzliches zur Rhythmik der mittelalterlichen Monodie," *Die Musikforschung*, 7 (1954), pp. 150–176.

Gennrich, F. *Lateinische Liedkontrafaktur; Eine Auswahl lateinischer Conductus mit ihren volkssprachigen Vorbildern*. Musikwissenschaftliche Studienbibliothek, 11. Darmstadt, 1956.

Gennrich, F. "Wer ist der Initiator der 'Modaltheorie?' Suum cuique," *Miscelánea en homenaje a Monseñor Higinio Anglés*. Vol. 1. Barcelona, 1958–1961, pp. 315–330.

Gérold, Théodore. *Histoire de la musique des origines à la fin du XIVe siècle*. Paris: Librairie Renouard, 1936.

Gérold, T. *La Musique au Moyen Age*. Paris: Champion, 1932.

Gleason, Harold (ed.). *Examples of Music before 1400*. Rochester, New York: Eastman School of Music of the University of Rochester, 1942.

Grocheo, Johannes de. *Concerning Music (De Musica)*. Edited and translated by Albert Seay. Colorado Springs, 1967.

Hughes, Dom Anselm (ed.). *Early Medieval Music up to 1300*. New Oxford History of Music. Vol. 2. London: Oxford University Press, 1954.

Husmann, Heinrich. "Zur Rhythmik des Trouvèregesanges," *Die Musikforschung*, 5 (1952), pp. 110–131.

Lommatzsch, Erhard. *Provenzalisches Liederbuch*. Berlin: Weidmann, 1917.

Ludwig, Friedrich. "Die Quellen der Motetten ältesten Stils, *Archiv für Musikwissenschaft*, 5 (1923), 185–315. rpt. in *Summa musicae medii aevi*, vol. 7. Edited by Friedrich Gennrich. Langen bei Frankfurt, 1961.

Ludwig, F. *Repertorium organorum recentioris et motetorum vetustissimi stili*. Vol. 1: *Catalogue raisonné der Quellen*. Part 1: *Handschriften in Quadrat-Notation*. 2nd edition, ed. Luther Dittmer. New York: Institute of Mediaeval Music, 1964.

Maillard, Jean. *Anthologie de chants de troubadours*. Nice: Georges Delrieu , 1967.

Parrish, Carl. *The Notation of Medieval Music*. New York, 1957, rpt. 1978.

Rohloff, Ernst (ed.). *Der Mensuraltraktat des Johannes de Grocheo*. Mediae Latinitatis musica, II. Leipzig, 1943.

Rokseth, Yvonne. *Polyphonies du XIIIe siècle, le manuscrit H.196 de la faculté de médicine de Montpellier*. 4 vols. Paris, 1935–1939.

Schrade, Leo. *Polyphonic Music of the Fourteenth Century*. Vol. 1. Monaco: Editions de L'oiseau-lyre, 1956.

Sesini, Ugo. *Le Melodie trobadoriche nel canzoniere provenzale della Biblioteca Ambrosiana R.71 sup*. Torino: Chiantore, 1942.

Sesini, U. *Musiche trobadoriche*. Naples, 1941.

Tiersot, B. *Histoire de la chanson populaire en France*. Paris, 1889.

Van der Werf, Hendrik, see Werf, Hendrik van der.

Waite, William G. *The Rhythm of Twelfth Century Polyphony*. Yale Studies in Music History, I. New Haven, 1954, rpt. Westport, 1973.

Werf, Hendrik van der. "Concerning the Measurability of Medieval Music," *Current Musicology*, 10 (1970), pp. 69–73.

Werf, H. van der. "Deklamatorischer Rhythmus in den Chansons der Trouvères," *Die Musikforschung*, 20 (1967), pp. 122–144.

Werf, H. van der. *The Chansons of the Troubadours and the Trouvères: A Study of the Melodies and their Relation to the Poems*. Utrecht: Oosthoek, 1972.

Werf, H. van der. "The Trouvère Chansons as Creations of a Notationless Musical Culture," *Current Musicology*, 1 (1965), pp. 61–68.

Werf, H. van der. *Trouvères Melodien, I : Blondel de Nesle, Gautier de Dargies, Chastelain de Coucy, Conon de Béthune, Gace Brulé*. Monumenta monodica medii aevi, XI. Kassel, 1977.

Wolf, Johannes. *Geschichte der Mensural-Notation von 1250 bis 1460*. Leipzig, 1904.

Wolf, J. "Die Musiklehre des Johannes de Grocheo," *Sammelbände der Internationalen Musikgesellschaft*, 1 (1899–1900), pp. 65–130.

Zingerle, Hans. *Tonalität und Melodieführung in den Klauseln der Troubadours- und Trouvèreslieder*. Tutzing: Schneider, 1958.

GUILHEM IX

Bezzola, Reto R. "Guillaume IX et les origines de l'amour courtois," *Romania*, 66 (1940), pp. 145–237.

Blackburn, James E. "A Study of the Poetics of Guillaume IX d'Aquitaine," Diss. Tulane University 1971. DAI 32 (1972), 6366A.

Blackburn, J. E. "William of Aquitaine: The Original Conteur?," *French Literature Series*, 2 (1975) [*The French Short Story*. Edited by Phillip Crant], pp. 155–159.

Bond, Gerald A. "The Uncourtly Poetry of the Count of Poitiers, William VII," Diss. Yale University 1973. DAI 34 (1974), 7221A.

Bond, G. A. "Philological Comments on a New Edition of the First Troubadour" [Rev. of Pasero], *Romance Philology*, 30 (1976), pp. 343–361.

Camproux, Charles. "Remarque sur la langue de Guilhem de Peitieus," *Mélanges offerts à Rita Lejeune*. Vol. 1. Gembloux: Duculot, 1969, pp. 67–84.

Chailley, J. "Les Premiers troubadours et les versus de l'école d'Aquitaine," *Romania*, 76 (1955), pp. 212–239.

Dronke, Peter. "Guillaume IX et courtoisie," *Romanische Forschungen*, 73 (1961), pp. 327–338.

Dumitrescu, Maria. "Èble II de Ventadorn et Guillaume IX d'Aquitaine," *Cahiers de civilisation médiévale*, 11 (1968), pp. 379–412.

Dumitrescu, M. "Les premiers troubadours connus et les origines de la poésie provençale," *Cahiers de civilisation médiévale*, 9 (1966), pp. 345–354.

Favati, Guido. "L'innovazione di Guglielmo IX d'Aquitania e un canto di Marbodo di Rennes," *Annales de l'Institut d'études occitanes*, 2 (1970), pp. 65–76.

Hanawalt, Emily Albu. "A Note on William IX," *Arion*, n.s. 3 (1976), pp. 490–492.

Jansen, Rudolf K. "Randbemerkungen zum ersten Troubadour und ersten Minnesänger," *Deutsche Viertel-jahrsschrift für Literaturwissenschaft und Geistesgeschichte*, 48 (1974), pp. 767–771.

Jeanroy, Alfred. *Les Chansons de Guillaume IX, duc d'Aquitaine (1071–1127)*. 2nd edition. Les Classiques français du moyen âge, 9. Paris: Champion, 1927.

Lejeune, Rita. "Formules féodales et style amoureux chez Guillaume IX d'Aquitaine," *Atti VIII Congresso Int. di Studi Romanzi, Firenze 1956*. Vol. 2. Florence: Sansoni, 1959, pp. 228–248.

Lejeune, R. "L'extraordinaire insolence du troubadour Guillaume IX d'Aquitaine," *Mélanges de langue et de littérature médiévales offerts à Pierre Le Gentil*. Paris: S.E.D.E.S., 1973, pp. 485–503.

Nichols, Stephen G., Jr. "*Canso → Conso*: Structures of Parodic Humor in Three Songs of Guilhem IX," *L'Esprit créateur*, 16 (1976), pp. 16–29.

Panzer, Friedrich. "Der älteste Troubadour und der erste Minnesinger," *Euphorion*, 40 (1939), pp. 133–145.

Pasero, Nicolò. *Guglielmo IX d'Aquitania: Poesie*. Modena: S.T.E.M—Mucchi, 1973.

Pfister, Max. "Die Sprache von Guilhem IX, Graf von Poitiers," *Mélanges de langues et de littératures romanes offerts à Carl Theodor Gossen*. Edited by Germán Colón and Robert Kopp. Bern: Marche Romane, 1976, pp. 715–735.

Pfister, M. "La langue de Guilhem IX, comte de Poitiers," *Cahiers de civilisation médiévale*, 19 (1976), pp. 91–113.

Pollman, Leo. "Dichtung und Liebe bei Wilhelm von Aquitanien," *Zeitschrift für romanische Philologie*, 78 (1962), pp. 326–357.

Rajna, Pio. "Guglielmo, conte di Poitiers, trovatore bifronte," *Mélanges de linguistique et de littérature offerts à M. Alfred Jeanroy*. Paris: Droz, 1928, pp. 349–360.

Spoerri, Theodore. "Wilhelm von Poitiers und die Anfänge der abendländischen Poesie," *Trivium*, 2 (1944), pp. 255–277. Reprinted in *Der provenzalische Minnesang: Ein Querschnitt durch die neuere Forschungsdiskussion*. Edited by Rudolf Baehr. Darmstadt: Wissenschaftliche Buchgesellschaft, 1967, pp. 175–197.

Storost, Joachim. "Textkritisches zu Wilhelm von Poitiers," *Saggi e ricerche in memoria di E. Li Gotti*. Vol. 3. Palermo, 1966, pp. 221–234.

Suchier, Walther. "Zur Chronologie der Lieder Wilhelms von Poitou," *Archiv für das Studium der neueren Sprachen und Literaturen*, 186 (1949), pp. 125–128.

Topsfield L. T. "The Burlesque Poetry of Guilhem IX of Aquitaine," *Neuphilologische Mitteilungen*, 69 (1968), pp. 280–302.

Topsfield, L. T. "Three Levels of Love in the Poetry of the Early Troubadours: Guilhem IX, Marcabru and Jaufre Rudel," *Mélanges de philologie romanes dédiés à la mémoire de Jean Boutière*. Edited by Irénée M. Cluzel and François Pirot. Vol. 1. Soledi, 1971, pp. 571–587.

Villard, François. "Guillaume IX d'Aquitaine et le concile de Reims de 1119," *Cahiers de civilisation médiévale*, 16 (1973), pp. 295–302.

GENERAL

Andreas Capellanus. *The Art of Courtly Love*. Translated by J. J. Parry. New York, 1941.

Anglade, Joseph. *Anthologie des troubadours*. Paris: E. DeBoccard, 1953.

Anglade, J. "La Doctrine grammaticale et poétique du 'gai savoir'," *Todd Memorial Volumes*. Edited by John D. Fitz-Gerald and Pauline Taylor. Vol. 1. New York: Columbia University Press, 1930, rpt. 1968, pp. 47–58.

Aubry, P. *Trouvères et troubadours*. New York: Cooper Square, 1969.

Belperron, Pierre. *La 'joie d'amour', contribution à l'étude des troubadours et de l'amour courtois*. Paris, 1948.

Bergin, Thomas G. and Raymond T. Hill. *Anthology of the Provençal Troubadours*. 2nd edition revised and enlarged. 2 vols. Yale Romanic Studies, Second Series, 23. New Haven: Yale University Press, 1973.

Bezzola, Reto R. *Les Origines et la formation de la littérature courtoise en Occident (500–1200)*. 5 vols. in 3. Paris: Champion, 1944–1963.

Blackburn, Paul. *Proensa: An Anthology of Troubadour Poetry*. Edited by George D. Economou. Berkeley: University of California Press, 1978.

Boase, Roger. *The Origin and Meaning of Courtly Love: A Critical Study of European Scholarship*. Manchester: Manchester University Press, 1977.

Bonner, Anthony. *Songs of the Troubadours*. New York: Schocken Books, 1972.

Briffault, Robert S. *Les Troubadours et le sentiment romanesque*. Paris: Editions du chêne, 1945. Translated into English as *The Troubadours*. Edited by Lawrence F. Koons. Bloomington: Indiana University Press, 1965.

Camproux, Charles. *Histoire de la littérature occitane*. 2nd edition. Paris: Payot, 1971.

Cavalcanti, Guido. *The Sonnets and Ballads of Guido Cavalcanti*. Translated by Ezra Loomis Pound. Boston: Small, Maynard and Co., 1912.

Chaytor, Henry John. *The Provençal Chanson de Geste*. London: Oxford University Press, 1946.

Chaytor, H. J. *The Troubadours*. Cambridge: Cambridge University Press, 1912.

Chaytor, H. J. *The Troubadours and England*. Cambridge: Cambridge University Press, 1923.

Chaytor, H. J. *The Troubadours of Dante*. Oxford: Clarendon Press, 1902.

Cropp, Glynnis M. *Le Vocabulaire courtois des troubadours de l'époque classique*. Publications romanes et françaises, 135. Geneva: Droz, 1975.

Diez, Friedrich. *Die Poesie der Troubadours*. 2nd edition. Edited by Karl Bartsch. Leipzig: J. A. Barth, 1883.

Diez, F. *Leben und Werke der Troubadours*. 2nd edition. Edited by Karl Bartsch. Leipzig: J. A. Barth, 1883.

Dronke, Peter. *Medieval Latin and the Rise of the European Love-Lyric*. 2 vols. Oxford: Oxford University Press, 1965–1966.

Dronke, P. *The Medieval Lyric*. 2nd edition. London: Hutchinson, 1978.

Ford, Ford Madox. *Provence: From Minstrels to the Machine*. London, 1935.

Frank, István. "Du rôle des troubadours dans la formation de la poésie lyrique moderne," *Mélanges de linguistique et de littérature romanes offerts à Mario Roques*. Vol. 1. Paris: Bade, 1950, pp. 63–81.

Frank, I. *Répertoire métrique de la poésie des troubadours*. 2 vols. Paris: Champion, 1953–1957.

Frings, Theodor. *Minnesinger und Troubadours*. Berlin: Akadamie-Verlag, 1949.

Gennrich, F. *Lo Gai Saber: 50 ausgewählte Troubadourlieder Melodien*. Musikwissenschaftliche Studien-Bibliothek, 18/19. Darmstadt, 1959.

Golden, Frederick. *Lyrics of the Troubadours and Trouvères*. New York: Doubleday, 1973.

Golden, F. "The Array of Perspectives in the Early Courtly Love Lyric," *In Pursuit of Perfection: Courtly Love in Medieval Literature*. Edited by Joan M. Ferrante and George D. Economou. Port Washington, New York: Kennikat Press, 1975, pp. 51–100.

Hueffer, Francis. *Troubadours: A History of Provençal Life and Literature in the Middle Ages*. London: Chatto and Windus, 1878.

Ibn Sina. "A Treatise on Love by Ibn Sina," translated by E. L. Fackenheim. *Medieval Studies*, 7 (1945), pp. 208–228.

Igly, France. *Troubadours et trouvères*. Paris: Seghers, 1960.

Jacoubet, Henri. *Le Compte de Tressan et les origines du genre troubadour*. Paris: Presses universitaires de France, 1923.

Jeanroy, Alfred. *La Poésie lyrique des troubadours*. 2 vols. Toulouse: E. Privat, 1934.

Jeanroy, A. *Les Origines de la poésie lyrique en France*. 3rd edition. Paris: Champion, 1925.

Köhler, Erich. "Observations historiques et sociologiques sur la poésie des troubadours," *Cahiers de civilisation médiévale*, 7 (1964), pp. 27–51.

Köhler, E. *Trobadorlyrik und höfischer Roman: Aufsätze zur französischen und provenzalischen Literatur des Mittelalters*. Neue Beiträge zur Literaturwissenschaft, 15. Berlin: Rütten and Loening, 1962.

Kolb, Herbert. *Der Begriff der Minne und das Entstehen der höfischen Lyrik*. Tübingen: Niemeyer, 1958.

Lazar, Moshe. *Amour courtois et 'fin'amors' dans la littérature du XIIe siècle*. Paris: Klincksieck, 1964.

Lewis, C. S. "Courtly Love," *The Allegory of Love: A Study in Medieval Tradition*. Oxford: Oxford University Press, 1936, pp. 1–43.

Lindsay, Jack. *The Troubadours and Their World of the Twelfth and Thirteenth Centuries*. London: F. Muller, 1976.

Marrou, Henri (Davenson, Henri). *Les Troubadours*. 2nd edition. Paris: Klincksieck, 1964.

McDougal, Stuart Y. *Ezra Pound and the Troubadour Tradition*. Princeton, New Jersey: Princeton University Press, 1972.

Mölk, Ulrich. *Trobar clus, trobar leu: Studien zur Dichtungstheorie der Trobadors*. Munich: Fink, 1968.

Moore, John C. *Love in Twelfth Century France*. Philadelphia: University of Pennsylvania Press, 1972.

Nichols, Stephen G., Jr. "Toward an Aesthetic of the Provençal *canso*," *The Disciplines of Criticism: Essays in Literary Theory, Interpretation, and History*. Edited by Peter Demetz. New Haven: Yale University Press, 1968, pp. 349–374.

Nykl, A. R. *Hispano-Arabic Poetry and its Relations with Old Provençal Troubadours*. Baltimore: J. H. Furst, 1946.

Panvini, Bruno. *Le Biographie Provenzali*. Florence: Olschki, 1952.

Paris, Gaston. *La Littérature française au Moyen Age*. 3rd edition. Paris, 1905.

Pollman, Leo. *Die Liebe in der hochmittelalterlichen Literatur Frankreichs: Versuch einer historischen Phänomenologie*. Analecta Romanica, 18. Frankfurt am Main: Klostermann, 1966.

Pound, Ezra Loomis. *Literary Essays*. Edited with an introduction by T. S. Eliot. Norfolk, Conn.: New Directions, 1954.

Pound, E. L. *Make It New*. New Haven: Yale University Press, 1935.

Pound, E. L. *Personae*. New York: New Directions, 1926.

Pound, E. L. *Quia pauper amavi*. London: The Egoist, 1919.

Pound, E. L. *The Cantos*. London: Faber, 1975.

Pound, E. L. *The Spirit of Romance*. New York: New Directions, 1953.

Pound, E. L. *The Translations*. Introduction by Hugh Kenner. London: Faber, 1970.

Press, Alan R. *Anthology of Troubadour Lyric Poetry*. Edinburgh Bilingual Library, 3. Edinburgh: Edinburgh University Press, 1971.

Rémy, Paul. *La Littérature provençale au Moyen Age*. Brussels: Office de Publicité. 1944.

Riquer, Martín de. *La Lírica de los trovadores*. Barcelona: Escuela de Filologia, 1948.

Riquer, M. de. *Los Trovadores: Historia, literaria, y textos*. Ensayos Planeta de lingüística y crítica literaria, 34. 3 vols. Barcelona: Editorial Planeta, 1975—.

Rossetti, Dante Gabriel. *Dante and his Circle*. London: Ellis and White, 1874.

Rossetti, D. G. *The Early Italian Poets*. London: Smith and Elder, 1861.

Rougemont, Denis de. *Love in the Western World*. Translated by Montgomery Belgion. Revised edition. New York: Harper and Row, 1974.

Snodgrass, W. D. *Six Troubadour Songs*. Providence, R. I. : Burning Deck Press, 1977.

Strónski, Stanislaw. *La Poésie et la réalité aux temps des troubadours*. Oxford: Clarendon Press, 1943.

Tavani, Giuseppe. *Repertorio Metrico della Lirica Galego-Portoghese*. Rome: Edizioni dell'Ateneo, 1967.

Terry, A. *A Literary History of Spain: Catalan Literature*. London: E. Benn, 1972.

Topsfield, L. T. *Troubadours and Love*. Cambridge: Cambridge University Press, 1975.

Valency, Maurice. *In Praise of Love: An Introduction to the Love-Poetry of the Renaissance*. New York: MacMillan, 1958.

Vincenti, Eleonora. *Bibliographia antica dei trovatori*. Milan: R. Ricciard, 1963.

Wilhelm, James J. *Seven Troubadours: The Creators of Modern Verse*. University Park, Pa.: Pennsylvania State University Press, 1970.

LANGUAGE

Anglade, Joseph. *Grammaire de l'ancien provençal ou l'ancienne langue d'oc: Phonétique et morphologie*. Paris: Klincksieck, 1921.

Bec, Pierre. *La Langue occitane*. Paris, 1963.

Grandgent, Charles Hall. *An Outline of the Phonology and Morphology of Old Provençal*. Revised edition. Boston: Heath, 1905.

Hamlin, Frank R., Peter T. Ricketts, and John Hathaway. *Introduction à l'étude de l'ancien provençal: Textes d'étude*. Geneva: Droz, 1967.

Levy, Emil. *Petit dictionnaire provençal-français*. 5th edition. Heidelberg: C. Winter, 1973.

Levy, E. *Provenzalisches Supplement-Wörterbuch: Berichtigungen und Ergänzungen zu Raynouard's Lexique roman*. 8 vols. Leipzig. 1894–1924.

Raynouard, François. *Lexique roman, ou Dictionnaire de la langue des troubadours*. 6 vols. Paris, 1838–1844.

Roncaglia, Aurelio. *La Lingua dei trovatori: Profilo di grammatica storica del provenzale antico*. Rome: Edizioni dell'Ateneo, 1965.

Index

199

LIST OF PLATES

Composed in Palatino type by Friedrich Typography of Santa Barbara. Printed on 70 lb. Sterling Litho Matte and Smythe Sewn bound by LithoCrafters of Chelsea, Michigan. Book designed and illustrated by Gary H. Brown. Production edited by Timothy Wardell.

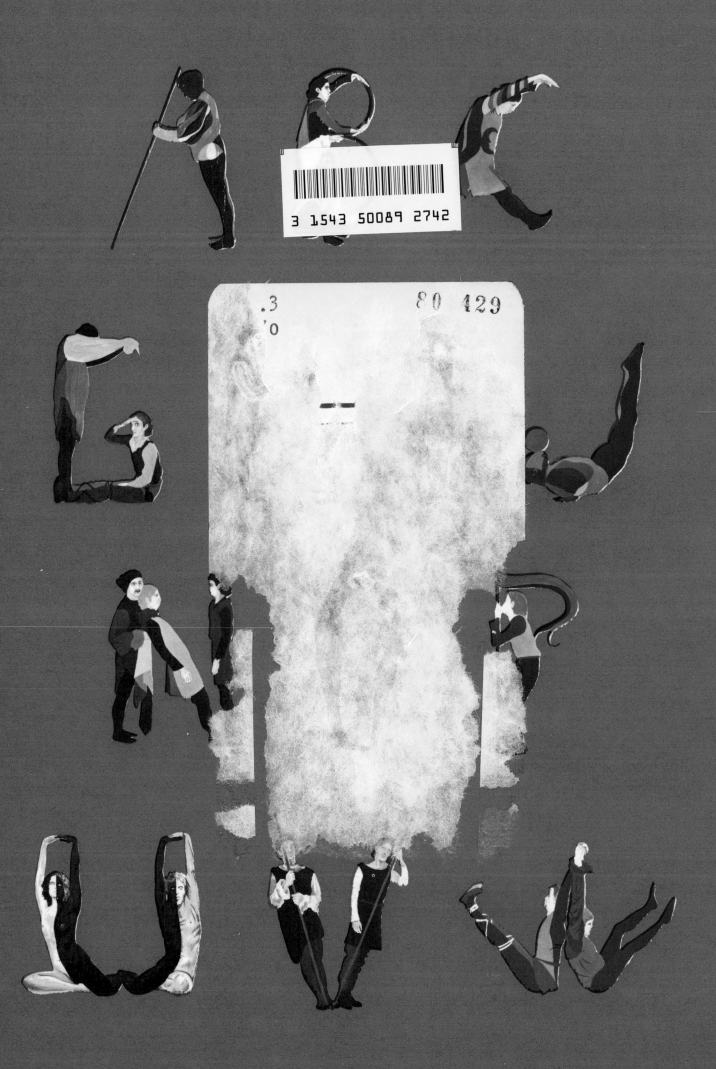